D0481498

A DOG OWNER'S GUIDE TO

THE DOBERMANN

Tetra Press

No. 16044

A DOG OWNER'S GUIDE TO

THE DOBERMANN

Jimmy Richardson

Photographs by Marc Henrie

A Salamander Book

© 1986 Salamander Books Ltd.,
Published in the USA by
Tetra Press,
3001 Commerce Street,
Blacksburg,
VA 24060

ISBN 1-56465-189-4

Credits

Editor: Tony Hall
Designer: Geoff Denney and Philip Gorton
Photographs: Marc Henrie
Illustrations: Ray Hutchins
Color origination: Rodney Howe Ltd and Kentscan
Typesetting: The Old Mill
Printed in Portugal

Contents

Author

An international show judge for many years, Jimmy Richardson is today
one of the experts on the Dobermann breed standard. He has been actively
involved in the breed since 1963 and has held a number of highly influential
posts within the breed society. He is past chairman of the Dobermann
breed council and is the breed representative at the Kennel Club.

**Please note that except for American references, the German
spelling of the breed name — Dobermann — has been used
throughout the book. For details of these spellings, see page 15.**

Veterinary Consultant

Trevor Turner qualified from the Royal Veterinary College, London, in 1958 and within a few months had set up a small animal practice at his home in Northolt, near London. He now runs an extensive small animal hospital. Trevor has always owned dogs and cats in multiplicity. Litters are planned and bred on an occasional basis.

An active member of many veterinary associations and past president of some, Trevor writes and speaks widely on a variety of topics connected with small animal practice. He believes that the role of the vet involves not only treatment of the patient but also intelligible communication with the owners, who should always feel free to question and discuss problems. Trevor was presented with the covered BSAVA Melton Award in 1988.

US Consultant

Hal Sundstrom, as president of Halamar Inc, publishers, of North Virginia, has been editing and publishing magazines on travel and pure-bred dogs since 1972. He is the recipient of six national writing and public excellence awards from the Dog Writer's Association of America, of which he is now president, and he is a past member of the Collie Club of America. He is now a delegate to the AKC representing the Collie Club of America.

Hal has an extensive background and enormous experience in the dog world as a breeder/handler/exhibitor, match and sweeps judge, officer and director of specialty and all-breed clubs, show and symposium chairman, and officer of the Arizona and Hawaii Councils of Dog Clubs.

Photographer

Marc Henrie began his career as a Stills man at the famous Ealing Film Studios in London. He then moved to Hollywood where he worked at MGM, RKO, Paramount and Warner Brothers, photographing the Hollywood greats: Humphrey Bogart, Edward G Robinson, Gary Cooper, Joan Crawford and Ingrid Bergman, to name a few. He was one of the last photographers to photograph Marilyn Monroe.

Later, after he had returned to England, Marc specialised in photographing dogs and cats, establishing an international reputation.

He has won numerous photographic awards, most recently the Kodak Award for the Best Animal Photograph and the Neal Foundation Award for Outstanding Photography of Animal Behaviour.

Marc is married to ex-ballet dancer, Fiona Henrie, who now writes and illustrates books on animals. They live in West London with their daughter Fleur, two King Charles Cavalier Spaniels and a cat called Topaz.

Author's acknowledgments

The author and editor would like to thank the following people for their invaluable help and support. Nick and Avril Munson for their work on the photo session for the training chapter. Ilio — Hawaii Dogs for supplying us with the photograph of 'Irish Fantasy' on page 71. Seymour Weiss for his additional consultative expertise. The Kennel Club for their permission to reproduce the Breed Standard. Finally, the author would also like to thank his mother, Mrs Daisy Richardson.

Please note that except for American references, the German spelling of the breed name — Dobermann — has been used throughout the book. For details of these spellings see page 15.

Introduction

If you already share your life with a Dobermann you will know just why the breed is one of the aristocrats of the dog world. Those of you that have not yet joined this elite society are missing out on one of the great joys of life.

Love and affection

What always surprises those owning a Dobermann for the first time is that it never wants to let you out of its sight. As a breed, they are extremely loving and crave affection at every opportunity, never wanting to be apart from you. They also have an uncanny way of knowing what you are going to do almost before you have decided to do it. When you take a Dobermann into the house it is like adopting a child, as it will very soon become another member of the family.

Being highly intelligent, the Dobermann is a quick learner, and is therefore easily trained to be a happily integrated member of the family. However, he is also clever enough to know what is worth learning and what is not. He is reluctant to do things which he considers do not have a worthwhile end result. He will also learn how much he can get away with and what each member of the family can do for him! Once you have had the pleasure of being owned by a Dobermann, you will realise that it is a breed with no equal.

Practical guidance

In writing this book I have attempted to give practical guidance and advice on most aspects of owning, training, showing and breeding Dobermanns. This is based on my many years of involvement with the breed and I am grateful to have been given this opportunity of passing on some of the knowledge that I have acquired to you. It is my sincere hope that this book will give the prospective Dobermann owner an insight into the full potential of these dogs, while at the same time serving as a useful guide to the beginner. I also hope that there are a few ideas that will be of some interest to the more experienced Dobermann owner. My only regret is that there are insufficient pages between the two covers to allow me to discuss a number of the issues raised more fully — many of the subjects such as breeding, training, showing and management could each be the subject of a complete book in their own right.

It is said in the world of dogs that the more you learn, the more you realize how much you don't know. What is certainly true is that the more you learn, the more you will be able to enjoy the company of your Dobermann and the better able you will be to look after him. It would be nice to think that a few Dobermanns in the world may lead better lives as a result of this book.

Left: *Jimmy Richardson with 'Sable', one of his own Dobermanns. As a breed, Dobes are loving and crave affection.*

Below: *It is easy to see why the Dobermann is universally acknowledged to be an aristocrat of the dog world.*

Section One

OWNING A DOBERMANN

Chapter One

A HISTORY

The Dobermann gained its name from Herr Louis Dobermann, who is generally given the credit for its creation, though there were a number of others who played an important part in its early development. Herr Dobermann is known to have been born in 1823 and to have worked as a municipal knacker, tax collector, part-time policeman and local dog-catcher in Apolda, in the state of Thuringia, Germany.

Even though the Dobermann is relatively modern, little is known about the specific breeds that Herr Dobermann used in his breeding programme. What is known is that he set out to create the perfect guard dog, believing that he could improve on those already existing.

It is believed that he started with the German Pinscher, which was then quite common. It is fairly certain that he also used the Rottweiler and the old smoothcoat, bob-tailed German Shepherd Dog (not to be confused with the modern GSD), as he is known to have owned both breeds. Other breeds are a little more speculative, but probably include the Weimaraner, the German Short-haired Pointer, the Hungarian Visla and the Manchester Terrier. It was the Manchester Terrier, then a larger dog than it is today, which introduced the black and tan colour scheme which is the recognised trade mark of the breed.

Other breeds were undoubtedly used in the early days of the Dobermann as attempts were made

Above: *A fine head study taken in 1910 of Bob v. Elfenfeld. Note the shape of the head and the fact that his ears are cropped.*

to continue its improvement. One which was known to have been used in about 1908 is the Greyhound, the influence of which can still be seen.

OFFICIAL RECOGNITION

The first Dobermann entry in the German stud-book was in 1893 and the breed grew in popularity rapidly over the next few years, becoming officially known as the Dobermannpincher in 1899. In this same year Otto Goeller, who played such a leading role in developing the breed after the death of Herr Dobermann, organised the National Dobermannpincher Club in Germany. A breed standard was drawn up and accepted by the German Kennel Club in 1900.

World War I from 1914-1918 was a time of great hardship and famine in much of Europe. This led to many of the best dogs being sent to America, where they were already becoming popular. The first Doberman Pinscher club in America was established in 1921.

The Dobermann did not reach Britain until much later. There is a record of one being exhibited at the Kennel Club show at the Crystal Palace in 1933 but it was not until about 1947 that they came to Britain in any significant numbers. These importations, by Fred and Julia Curnow and Lionel Hamilton-Renwick, were initially from Germany, Holland and Switzerland, and later from America. It is from these early imports that the breed became established, though a number of later imports, principally from America, have helped it to reach its present high standard.

The spelling

It is interesting to note that in Britain the German spelling of the breed, 'Dobermann', is retained and the word 'Pinscher' dropped, whereas in America the second 'n' has been dropped and the 'Pinscher' retained, giving Doberman Pinscher.

THE USES OF THE BREED

Herr Dobermann set out initially to create the perfect guard dog and this is still the main function with which the breed is associated. The early Dobermanns almost certainly had an aggressive and vicious temperament but the Americans bred out much of these traits, producing an amenable, intelligent working dog. Even today, the continental Dobermanns tend to have sharper temperaments than the American or British dogs.

The Dobermann undoubtedly still retains the reputation amongst much of the general public of being a very fierce guard dog. This is

Below: *The years pass and the breed develops. This 1924 portrait is of a German dog Claus v. Sigalsburg.*

reinforced to a considerable extent by the use of Dobermanns in films, particularly in America, where they are usually typecast as being fierce, aggressive guard dogs. What the public does not realise, however, is that the dogs are playing a part just the same as the human actors. Nevertheless, it is this respect for the breed's reputation that makes a Dobermann in the house such an excellent deterrent. No one with any sense will break into a house knowing that there is a Dobermann inside, since however amenable it may actually be it will always bark when someone enters the gate — and many Dobermanns still take a dim view of uninvited guests.

Intelligence

The Dobermann's great intelligence, good nose and turn of speed make it an excellent breed for many other purposes. Dobermanns were used as war dogs by the Germans in World War I and by many countries in World War II. As

might be expected, they were deployed extensively as guard dogs, the Germans using them to guard their prisoner-of-war camps. They were also used on the battlefield, where they carried messages attached to their collars or, on some occasions, first-aid to wounded soldiers in advance of medical help being provided. Their excellent powers of smell were put to good use in detecting people buried under the rubble of bombed buildings.

It is also recorded that Dobermanns were used by the Germans and the Russians as anti-tank dogs. They were trained to take food from the underside of tanks and were then sent towards the enemy tanks with explosives tied on to their backs. As they went under the tanks the explosives were detonated, blowing the dog, the tank and its occupants to pieces.

Police dogs

The Dobermann is still popular with the police and armed forces in a number of countries, particularly those where it has the opportunity to track and do man-work (attack-work). The majority of police work in Britain tends to be of the routine

Below: *A German bitch from the 1930s in characteristic position. This is Jessy v.d. Sonnenhoehe photographed in 1934.*

patrolling kind, which makes the German Shepherd Dog, with its 'willing to please' temperament, amenability to training and thicker all-weather coat, more suitable as a working dog. In a number of countries, however, the Dobermann's true potential is fully exploited and they are used extensively as police dogs.

Over the years, I have come across Dobermanns used for a wide variety of purposes. A number have made excellent gundogs, learning very quickly which birds to put up. They are also very effective retrievers, for which task they have surprisingly soft mouths. More than once, I have come across them being used by farmers to herd cattle and sheep and I even know of one which is used to track deer after they have been hit by traffic on the main roads through a forest — an event which is, unfortunately, an all too frequent occurrence.

A FAMILY DOG

As we have already seen, the Dobermann is an excellent guard dog in the home and an excellent deterrent to burglars. While this is largely a result of the breed's reputation there are many Dobermanns who would attack an uninvited guest, even if its owners regard it as very softhearted. The ideal temperament is for the dog to deter people from coming into the house, but to welcome them once you bring them in. The Dobermann has an uncanny knack of knowing who is and who is not allowed into the house. This is important to him, as he considers it to be his.

In addition to guarding the house your Dobermann will also guard your car, and any other possessions within his territory. He will also guard the members of your family, both in the house and when out walking. Having a Dobermann with you certainly gives you a feeling of security.

You need have no fear of keeping a Dobermann if you have small children about the place, as he will simply see them as something else for him to keep an eye on. However, you will need to train your children to respect your dog, possibly more than you will need to train the dog himself. When a dog bites a child, it is very often because the child has teased or even hurt the dog rather than because the dog is vicious. It may be necessary to watch your Dobermann when he is suddenly confronted with a child if he is not used to them, as he is likely to be wary of anything that he does not understand. Dobermanns that are brought up from puppyhood with children rarely cause any problems.

Below: *The Powerful head and neck of German Dobermann Prins Favoriet v.d. Koningstad. Here in beautiful study.*

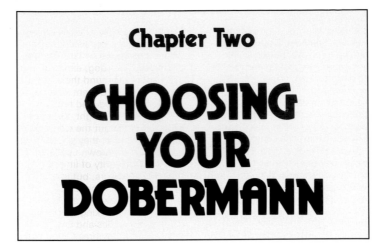

Chapter Two

CHOOSING YOUR DOBERMANN

IS THE DOBERMANN FOR YOU?

As a breed, the Dobermann has everything going for it. With its short, fine coat and stylish outline, it is certainly one of the aristocrats of the dog world. It's loyalty and faithfulness make it a loving and reliable companion; its superior intelligence makes it an easy dog to train; its inbuilt guarding instinct makes it the ideal dog to protect the home and to deter any but the most determined or the foolhardy from intruding into what very quickly becomes its territory. Before you decide that the Dobermann is the dog for you, you should first stop and consider whether you are a suitable person to own one. Taking a dog of any breed into your home involves accepting certain commitments and obligations, which may be seen as the price you have to pay for the pleasure of owning a dog.

The Dobermann is a large, active dog which needs daily exercise in order to maintain physical fitness and to prevent mental boredom. He also requires a garden, which will need to be securely fenced to prevent him from wandering beyond his boundaries. While he is not a breed that strays by nature, he does like to be involved in anything that is happening in the vicinity of his home. While he may well have no evil intentions, the

sight of a Dobermann roaming loose is likely to make you unpopular with your neighbours.

He is an extremely intelligent dog who learns very quickly. This means that not only will he learn things to his own advantage, but he will soon discover what he can get away with and how far he can push you. Like most of the guarding breeds, the Dobermann has a low flashpoint and will require little provocation to fight other dogs. This means that you will not be able to let him run loose in public parks when there are other dogs.

Caring for a puppy

Looking after a puppy will be an almost full-time occupation, certainly for the first few weeks. It is likely to be active, inquisitive and, if not kept fully occupied,
mischievous as well. As they grow up, Dobermann puppies can become very boisterous, self-willed, destructive towards furniture and carpets and, if not properly controlled and trained, disobedient as well. There will need to be someone at home all the time as the puppy will need to be fed three times each day and let out into the garden for toilet purposes at regular intervals.

A puppy that is left on its own all day is likely to become destructive through boredom; noisy through being left alone, thereby possibly causing neighbour problems; dirty in the house, through not being let outside when necessary; and neurotic through being left alone for long periods of time.

In short, to own a Dobermann you need to be physically capable of controlling and exercising it, mentally capable of anticipating and reacting to the actions of a highly intelligent, alert dog, financially capable of feeding a big dog and have the patience to rear a puppy. If you really believe that you measure up to these exacting requirements and that you will make a suitable Dobermann owner, then it is time to start looking for your puppy

WHERE TO BUY YOUR PUPPY

There is an old adage which says 'Buy from a Breeder'. This is not simply propaganda put out by the breeders in order to enhance their sales, but something that merits serious consideration. Breeders are generally concerned about the well-being of the breed and the quality of stock that they produce. They are likely to have been in the breed for some time or at least have some knowledge about the background of their bitches and the dogs they use at stud. This means

that they are likely to be able to breed to a more consistent type than the one-bitch owner who uses a particular stud dog, either because it lives round the corner or because it is the current winning dog. Puppies produced from such matings maybe all right, but there is less certainty about the type or temperament that they will have once they have grown up.

The vast majority of litters bred are not by breeders, but by people who own one or more bitches. Many of these owners are very conscientious, seeking to produce top quality puppies and taking great pride in what they breed. Many have good quality bitches with good pedigrees and take great care in selecting their stud dogs. The result is that they are able to produce good-quality puppies. Equally, there are some breeders who fall short of the high standards that we would all like to see, and to whom the quantity of puppies is more important than their quality. These points should be borne in

Below: *The result of a black bitch and fawn dog mating; all four Dobe colours in one litter, black, brown, blue and fawn.*

mind before you rush out and buy the first attractive-looking puppy that is offered to you.

Finding a breeder

There are a number of ways of finding out where there are puppies for sale. Litters are often advertised in the local press, in the specialist canine press or in advertisement magazines. It may also be worth your while to contact your national Kennel Club, who will supply you with a list of breeders. You will then be able to contact someone on that list and seek information on available litters from them. Another source of information is from one of the Dobermann breed clubs. They will not only be able to put you in touch with reputable breeders in your area, but may be able to give you details of litters of which they are aware. Many breeders will have information on litters sired by their stud dogs, though they may not always be able to guarantee the quality of such litters, particularly if they have not seen them or do not know how well they have been reared.

An alternative approach is to reserve a puppy from a reputable kennel, making it quite clear for what purpose you require the puppy, e.g. for showing or as a family pet. Even if the kennel cannot provide you with a puppy, it may be able to give you details of litters from other breeders which are from well-established bloodlines or from high-quality stock from which you are more likely to obtain the puppy you want. You will only be reserving an option. Don't commit yourself until you have seen the puppy at about six to eight weeks of age and you are sure that you like what you see. No reputable breeder will object to you taking this stance.

Some breeders will ask you for a deposit if you make a definite commitment. This is perfectly reasonable, but you should not pay a deposit until you are sure that you want the puppy, possibly after having seen it. The deposit requested is generally about 10 per cent of the purchase price.

Remember, though, that you will lose this deposit should you change your mind and at the last moment refuse to accept the puppy.

The best advice, therefore, is to look at any litters which seem interesting. It is advisable always to do this by arrangement, as people do not always welcome visitors dropping in uninvited. Don't be tempted to buy the first puppy you see — all puppies are lovely when they are young. If necessary look at several litters, but only commit yourself once you are sure that you have found a puppy which you really want and which appears suitable for your purpose.

If you merely require a pet, there are a number of rescue organizations which may be able to help you.

WHICH IS THE PUPPY FOR YOU?

The decision whether to buy a dog or a bitch is very much a matter of personal choice. A bitch is slightly smaller than a dog, is generally less

aggressive and less dominant and therefore possibly easier to handle. It will, of course, come into season twice a year, so will need to be kept out of circulation during these periods. The dog is the more dominant animal, though both sexes can fight if they want to do so. Both are equally loving and affectionate, equally easy to train and can also be equally self-willed and obstinate.

You should also have a clear idea of why you want a Dobermann and what you want it to do for you. The majority of people merely want a Dobermann as a family pet which will also guard the house. If you have any aspirations towards showing your dog you will need to ensure that it has the correct conformation as well as being a pleasant family dog. If you hope to breed from your dog in due course, be it a dog or a bitch, you should choose a good specimen of the breed that comes from a reputable bloodline. Breeding from poor-quality or defective stock does neither your nor the breed any credit. If you are hoping to work your dog, either in obedience or working trials, you should select a puppy that is outgoing and has a happy disposition, but you can forgive minor faults which may prevent it from being a successful show dog.

You should acquire your puppy any time after it is seven weeks old. Some breeders prefer to hold them until eight weeks, but no reputable breeder should let them go at under seven weeks except in very exceptional circumstances. The majority of puppies are sold at between seven and 12 weeks of age, but do not be worried about acquiring puppies older than this; puppies of six or seven months may be big in size but they are still babies and will normally settle

Below: *Your choice of puppy should be made with certain preferences in mind, such as dog or bitch and colour of coat.*

down happily in a new home within a few days. Breeders occasionally run puppies on in order to ascertain their show potential, then sell the ones not selected at about this age. You should not be asked to pay extra for an older puppy unless it is an exceptionally good one, and you will reap the benefit of acquiring a half-grown dog. You will need to be careful that this is not a disadvantage in that the puppy has been badly reared. With an older puppy you will also get a far better idea of its appearance and temperament as an adult.

Apart from its looks and its personality, you should carefully inspect the physical condition of the puppy. It should have a clean skin, be well-covered (even on the fat side), have clean, clear eyes and appear to be in good health. Inevitably, some puppies will be better reared than others and it may well be that where the puppy is healthy but is on the thin side you will soon be able to rectify that by giving it the individual attention it has lacked. If it appears unhealthy, in that it looks dull and lethargic or has spots on its head, forechest or tummy, be wary. While you may be able to correct the condition fairly quickly, you would be better advised to say no. You should not have to take on a financial liability when you purchase your puppy — leave that to the breeder.

Temperament
Whether you are looking for a family pet and guard or a showdog, it is essential that you have a dog with a good temperament. You want one that is loving and affectionate to the members of your family, barks when anyone comes on to your premises, yet accepts people you bring in to the house. You do not need an aggressive dog to guard your home. An aggressive dog is a liability, since you need to be sure that any well-intentioned visitors coming into your house are not at risk. With an aggressive dog, you are never at ease — you are always expecting that it may be about to do something antisocial.

There are differing opinions as to what constitutes 'good temperament'. Some people want their dog to show aggression towards anyone coming on to the premises. This is fair enough, as long as such people are able to control their dogs at all times. The problem often comes later, however, when they breed puppies which inherit the same aggressive tendencies and sell them to normal family homes where such a temperament cannot be controlled. Such dogs not only get the breed a bad name but tend to be the ones that become homeless, often ending up in the hands of rescue organizations. It is also worth remembering that even the police and the army do not really want aggressive dogs. They much prefer

those with steady temperaments which can be properly controlled and trained to be aggressive on command.

It is not always possible to tell what the eventual temperament of a dog will be when you see it as an eight-week-old puppy. However, you should look for a puppy which comes to you, shows a lively interest in everything around it, does not object to being picked up and petted and shows some affection towards you. Some puppies may not come to you immediately but will hold back and size you up first. This should not put you off, as it does not mean that the puppy will necessarily grow up to be nervous. You should be wary of one that runs and hides and shows fear or dislike of you.

Above: *Look carefully at the puppies before choosing. They should be outward going and in a good, well-covered condition.*

Such a puppy may well grow up to be loving, loyal and faithful to you, but may always be nervous of strangers, unhappy at going out in public and wary of visitors to your house. While it will not necessarily be aggressive, life can be more difficult for you and the dog, particularly if you are part of an extrovert and social family.

Even if your eight week old puppy appears to have a sound stable temperament, there is no guarantee that this will remain as it gets older. The true temperament does not develop until about five or

23

six months old. It is helpful, therefore, if you can see the parents or indeed any other close relatives as, while the puppy may not inherit the same temperament as the parents, it will certainly give you a useful pointer. Ask to see the mother (the dam) and, if you are unsure, enquire who is the father (the sire) and make arrangements to see him too. You do not have to commit yourself to purchasing a puppy just because you have been to see it. If you are not certain, say so. No reputable breeder will be offended. Seeing the parents will also give you a good indication of what the puppy may look like when it grows up. You must also remember that the eventual temperament of the dog will depend to a large extent on the way that it is brought up. It will be a combination of what it inherits and its environment.

CHOOSING A SHOW PUPPY

If you are interested in showing your puppy you will need to ensure that it not only has a good temperament but has good conformation as well. There is nothing magic about a show dog. Many family pets are well up to show standard, whether or not they are actually shown, and equally the majority of show dogs are also family pets. Obviously if you hope to show your dog you should try to purchase a puppy which has the greatest show potential. To do this successfully requires a great deal of experience and even then is not always easy.

You may wish to ask a reputable kennel or breeder to help you by selecting a puppy with show potential. In any litter of puppies, there will be some which have more of this than others. The dividing line is often very fine, and it may be a matter of purely subjective judgement. It is an advantage if you can have the 'pick of the litter', as this will enhance your chances of a good puppy. A breeder will often keep a puppy back for breeding or showing, but may pick the wrong one and let the best one go. Beware, however, as there are often no puppies of show quality in a litter.

Do not expect to buy a champion; these are few and far between. Not only would you need

Below: *A fawn puppy 'Izzy' at ten weeks, beginning early show-training using the top and tail method of presentation.*

to be lucky enough to acquire a dog of exceptionally good conformation, but it would require a considerable amount of dedication in terms of training and travelling to shows to achieve the ultimate accolade.

In assessing the show potential of a puppy, what you are trying to do is to compare its conformation, construction and temperament against the breed standard. At the same time, you are assessing what the puppy will look like as an adult dog. To do this, you will need to stand each puppy in turn on a table-top, just as if you were presenting it to a judge. It may take a few minutes to persuade a puppy to submit to being stood up on a table but once it understands that no-one is going to hurt it, it usually gives way.

What should you look for?

Having got your puppy standing four square in front of you, you should look initially to judge if it is pleasing to the eye. You should see in miniature a well-balanced, sound dog. Look for a well boned puppy with straight front legs and tight feet. Don't worry about the knobbly knees — these are simply the growth points and will eventually disappear. Look for a deep chest down to the level of the elbows and check that the latter are held tightly to the side of the body. Shallow chests and loose elbows should be avoided. Look for a good lay-back of shoulder, giving a good reach of neck and a clean flow-through from the neck into a strong, level topline, and for a high tail-set. The tail should be a continuation of the topline and not be set at a lower level. There should be an adequate length and bend of stifle, and the hocks should be parallel. The mouth should be sound, in that the teeth of the upper jaw should close in front of but close to the teeth of the lower jaw. You should also check that the eyes are not too light in colour, that the head is generally well-proportioned, and that if it is a male puppy it is entire, which is to say that both testicles

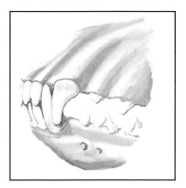

Above: *Your puppy should have a mouth with a scissor bite; the top teeth fitting over the lower.*

are apparent in the scrotum.

There are a number of things about which you will not be able to form too firm a judgement. While you can spot coarse heads and bad head planes, you cannot tell the eventual head shape as the head continues to pull out as the puppy grows. Eye colour will often appear light in a puppy but usually darkens over the next few months. Don't be too put off by a short neck, as long as the shoulder placement appears to be correct and the puppy is well-balanced overall; the neck will often pull out in proportion to the remainder of the dog. Fronts can be difficult to assess; if the front feet turn out only slightly, they may straighten as the puppy develops, though possibly not until six to nine months of age. If the turning front feet are associated with loose elbows be more cautious, as the two faults may indicate faulty construction rather than lack of development. Avoid a puppy with a bad mouth, as the second teeth will invariably also be wrong. On the other hand a good puppy bite does not always guarantee that the second teeth will be correctly placed — this is a gamble that you will have to take. Don't be misled by those who tell you that a puppy with a shallow chest is acceptable as it will drop later. If the chest is shallow at eight weeks, it will be shallow at eight months.

Chapter Three

FEEDING AND CARE

FEEDING

When you acquire your puppy he may be on three, four or even five meals per day — the diet sheet that you receive from the breeder will give you details. You should continue feeding the same way initially, then gradually change the diet or the feeding routine if you wish. There is no right or wrong way to feed your dog, as long as you follow certain basic rules and use your common sense.

Aim to get your puppy on to three meals per day as soon as you can — a main meal both morning and evening and a light, nutritional midday meal. At about five months, discontinue the latter. Continue the morning and evening meals until about 10 months of age, when the morning meal can be dropped, and the conventional one meal per day routine established. If your dog is thin or needs two meals per day in order to maintain weight, continue with two meals per day for as long as necessary.

Use either meat and biscuit or a complete manufactured feed for the main meals. Buy only good quality meat such as beef, ox-cheek, tongue or neck-pieces (either fresh or frozen). Tripe is an excellent meat to use and is readily available ground in frozen blocks. Some fat in the diet is necessary, but avoid feeding too much, and do not give

your dog over-rich meat such as horsemeat or pork.

Choose good quality plain wheatmeal biscuit and soak it before use, either with hot water or with the gravy from the meat. Use just sufficient to moisten the biscuit to a crumbly consistency and then stir in the meat, either ground or as small chunks. If you feed it raw, ensure that it is fresh and check that it is not causing diarrhoea, which is not uncommon with Dobermanns. Cooked meat is preferable, as it poses less risks and provides gravy with which to soak the biscuit, making it more apppetizing. It only needs to be lightly boiled in water with a pinch of added salt.

Adult dogs need a balance of about one-third meat, two-thirds biscuit; for growing puppies or whelping bitches the protein content can be increased slightly, though care must be taken not to feed puppies too high a level of protein.

COMPLETE FOODS

A wide variety of complete foods are now manufactured. These either consist of the individual ingredients mixed in the bag or are precooked and extruded into pellets. The various brands vary considerably in quality, so you should be prepared to try different kinds until you find one that suits your dog. Whichever type you use, make sure that you always soak it with hot water (without making it sloppy) before using it. Not only will this make the food more digestible but it will reduce the risk of bloat, which is commonly caused by dry food. The precooked pellet form products are preferable, as there is less risk of scouring from insufficient soaking of the meat powders which are used in some products. Avoid those containing excessive amounts of flaked maize; while this is excellent for putting on substance Dobermanns tend to develop an allergy to it, though this often becomes evident only after using the food for several months. The allergy will manifest itself as a rash of spots, either along the back or on the chest and tummy.

The complete foods are not only very convenient to use but provide a balanced diet in that they contain specified amounts of protein, carbohydrate, fats and oils, as well as all the vitamins, minerals and trace elements that a dog requires. Dobermanns generally do well on these foods, with a protein content of 20 – 27 per cent being most suitable. Do not alter the balance by giving extra protein and do not add vitamin supplements 'in case the dog needs them' – this will not only be wasteful but may even be harmful.

Canned foods
A wide range of canned dog foods are now available. They vary considerably in price and in quality but generally you get what you pay for, so stick to a well-known or recommended brand. Many Dobermanns have sensitive tummies and will develop diarrhoea if fed on canned foods, so be prepared. Canned food is not adequate as a regular diet for a Dobermann, though it is very useful as an occasional feed. A can of meat may be used instead of fresh meat and mixed with the soaked biscuit. It is advisable for your Dobermann to become accustomed to canned meat, as there may be occasions when fresh meat is not available.

Quantity
The quantity of food your dog needs will clearly depend on the nutritional value of the food and his individual requirements. As a rough guide, a puppy of two to three months should eat about 1lb (450g) of prepared food at each of his two main meals. This should be increased to 1½lb (700g) food up to four months old and 2lb (1kg) at six months.

Precise quantities can be found by trial and error; an adult male on one meal per day may well need 3lb (1.4g) prepared weight, a female about 2½lb (1.1kg).

Below: *A pellet-type of complete feed, soaked and ready in a stainless steel bowl. Quantities are checked by weighing.*

The midday meal for puppies up to about five months should be light but nutritious, such as egg custard, milk pudding or rice pudding. As a rough guide to serving, this meal should weigh about 1lb (450g).

Always ensure that your Dobermann has access to a plentiful supply of fresh, clean drinking water. This should be changed daily. A metal bowl is an ideal container; scrub it out regularly, particularly if it is left outside in summer, in order to remove the algae which will grow on it. Dobermanns will often carry their water bowl around with them or knock it over, so it may be necessary to hang up the bowl with a length of chain.

Your Dobermann should have his own dinner bowl, preferably of stainless steel and with a capacity of about 5 pints (3 litres). China or glass dishes are liable to be broken and enamel chips easily, particularly if your Dobermann carries his bowl around with him. Always wash the bowl after each meal, making sure that you rinse off any residual washing-up liquid. Detergent left on dishes can be harmful to the digestive system of dogs just as much as to humans.

Titbits should not constitute the main part of the diet, as they will almost certainly be inadequate, but they represent an important social part of the dog's need to share his master's food. The giving of titbits will not do any harm as long as you use common sense. Most Dobermanns will eat almost anything from the table and are particularly partial to fruit.

ADDITIVES

There is a wide range of vitamin and mineral supplements available for both growing puppies and adult dogs. By and large, most people give far too many such additives. If a dog is fed on a properly balanced diet the use of vitamin supplements is of no value, represents unnecessary expenditure and may prove harmful. This is particularly

true if you are feeding one of the 'complete' manufactured dog foods. There may be times, however, when the discriminating use of supplements may prove useful to you.

Calcium

Additional calcium to help the growing puppy to develop strong bones and teeth is generally accepted as being necessary, however this is best given in the form of calcium and phosphorous powder, with added vitamins A and D, in powder or tablet form. This is more necessary with a meat and biscuit diet than with a manufactured complete food. The dose depends on the size of the puppy and the precise product you use, but the manufacturer will provide you with a guide which should be followed (not exceeded!). This calcium supplement should be given up to about nine months of age. Beware of giving calcium in other forms, except under veterinary supervision. Liquid (colloidal) calcium or even calcium injections may be appropriate in some circumstances, for example when a puppy does not appear to be absorbing calcium properly and the front legs are bending badly. Given indiscriminately, however, serious consequences can arise.

Bonemeal is also frequently advocated for growing puppies. This is a good source of calcium and phosphorous, but again care must be taken not to give excess amounts and to ensure that it is fresh and is kept dry so as to avoid any risk of salmonella.

Vitamins A and D

Vitamin A plays an important role in the production and maintenance of skin, tissue and bone. Vitamin D is necessary for the absorption of calcium, so a vitamin D deficiency in a puppy would lead to soft bones and rickets. Being fat-soluble, vitamins A and D are stored in the body, so if excessive amounts are fed over a period of time they can build up to dangerous proportions. Excess vitamin D, when coupled with high levels of calcium, will result in bone deformity and calcification of the soft tissue, while an excess of vitamin A causes bone malformation.

Cod liver oil is a rich source of vitamins A, D and E. You should not give this to your puppy, and even an adult dog should only be allowed a small quantity about once per week during the winter months.

Vitamin E
Vitamin E is most readily available as wheatgerm capsules. As one of the functions of this vitamin is to help improve fertility, it is often recommended that it should be given to stud dogs and to bitches for a few weeks before mating.

Vitamins B and C
Vitamin B is best obtained as 'vitamin B compound' tablets which contain a selection of the B vitamins. They are relatively inexpensive and are beneficial to coat and skin.

Vitamin C is normally obtained as ascorbic acid tablets and is a useful winter additive. Again, this is beneficial to skin and coat. The addition of vitamins B and C to the diet is strongly recommended for the care of blues and fawns.

A number of brands of yeast tablets are available. They are basically a vitamin-rich yeast compound in tablet form, with the main vitamin being B. These can be given each day, increasing the number of tablets as the puppy grows. Even if these are not strictly necessary, they will not do any harm and your dog will enjoy them.

It is a good idea to give your dog a tablespoonful of vegetable cooking oil on his dinner occasionally. This will help keep the skin moist and put a shine on the coat. A lump of margarine is a useful alternative. You should consider giving this extra oil if the coat appears harsh, dry and scurfy, as it may be that he is not getting enough oil or fat in his diet.

Seaweed extract in tablet or powder form is a rich source of iodine, which is very useful for improving pigmentation. If given daily over a period of several months it will darken the tan markings and is particularly useful for darkening the coats of brown dogs, especially where they have lightened to a ginger colour in older age. However, seaweed will only enhance the dog's natural colour and it will not induce a dark coat if the dog's natural colour is a light one. There is no apparent risk from giving excess amounts.

Below: *Feeding a large number of dogs needs organisation and method. Note how each dinner is labelled to avoid confusion.*

WORMING

Your puppy should have been treated for roundworms at least twice before you acquire him. Check from the breeder whether or not this has been done and, if it has not, worm him as soon as possible. Otherwise, worm him again at about 12 – 14 weeks of age, as it is often difficult to be sure that all the worms have been removed. The number of worm tablets required for each dose will depend on the weight of your dog, but your vet will give you the appropriate dose.

The tablets should always be given with the main meal. You can either crush them and sprinkle them on the dinner or put them directly

Feeding and care

in the dog's mouth. If your dog has worms they will appear with the faeces some 12–24 hours later and in this case you should worm him again in about two weeks. Thereafter, do it every six months as a matter of routine.

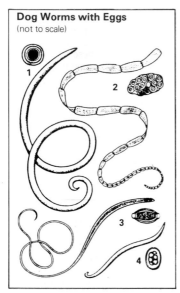

Dog Worms with Eggs
(not to scale)

Above: *Four types of parasite:*
1 Roundworm (Toxocara canis)
2 Tapeworm (Dipylidium canium)
3 Whipworm (Trichuris vulpis)
4 Hookworm (Ancylostoma caninum)

Tapeworms
Dobermanns may get tapeworms. They are harder to remove than roundworms, since their heads are attached to the wall of the intestine. The flea is an essential intermediary in the life-cycle of the tapeworm; eggs shed by the dog are swallowed by the fleas, in which they hatch. If the fleas are subsequently killed and eaten by the dog the worm larvae are released into the intestine, where they mature into tapeworms, thus beginning the whole cycle again.

You should not worm for tapeworms unless you suspect that your dog is infected. Symptoms are hair loss around the eyes, lack of

substance, ravenous appetite and a general loss of condition. You will also see individual segments of worm which have been shed – these will look like grains of rice in the faeces. Ask your vet for the appropriate remedy and administer in accordance with his instructions.

There are a number of other parasitic worms which dogs may occasionally have, but these would best be identified by means of a faecal analysis.

VACCINATION

Puppies derive some protective antibodies from their mothers, initially from the mother's blood supply while still in the uterus but mainly from the first milk or colostrum. These will be to the diseases from which she has suffered or has been vaccinated against. The higher her level of protection, the higher will be the level of maternal antibody protection acquired by the puppies. This will gradually decline until the puppies have no antibody protection remaining (normally at about 12 weeks of age).

You should therefore vaccinate your puppy when he is about 12 weeks old, when he should react to the vaccine to create his own antibodies and gain the protection he needs. Any vaccine given before 12 weeks is likely to be ineffective, as the puppy will not respond to it due to its maternal antibody protection. The exception is a puppy which did not receive any of its mother's colostrum within the first few days of birth and therefore is likely to have a much reduced level of maternal protection. As a precaution, such puppies should be given an additional vaccination at six weeks old as well as the conventional one at 12 weeks. Keep your puppy away from other dogs (and from areas used by other dogs) until two weeks after he has been vaccinated, in order to give the vaccines time to take effect. The vaccination will normally cover the five major canine diseases of hardpad, distemper, hepatitis, leptospirosis and parvovirus. These are generally given as one injection, or possibly as two injections at 12 and 14 weeks, depending upon the manufacturer's instructions and the vet's preference.

Antibodies

Antibody levels for parvovirus tend to be higher, which means that a puppy's maternal protection against this will take longer to decline. Consequently, the puppy is less likely to respond to the 12 week vaccination. As a breed, the Dobermann has been found to be particularly prone to this problem, so you should re-vaccinate your puppy for parvovirus at six months of age as a precaution.

Check with your vet that the hepatitis vaccine is dead (inactivated). Dobermanns are very susceptible to live hepatitis vaccine and have been known to develop hepatitis from it, sometimes with fatal results. Whether live or dead parvovirus vaccine should be used is a subject of much discussion.

Live vaccine is generally considered to be longer lasting and to be safe, since it uses the feline panleucopenia virus which is harmless to dogs but at the same time has the ability to trigger off antibody protection.

Vaccines are now available for kennel cough and coronavirus, which is similar to parvovirus but generally only affects puppies and is not as lethal. These are currently in more general use in the USA than in Britain.

Rabies vaccine is not generally available in Britain except for dogs being exported or imported and then only on licence from the Ministry of Agriculture, Food and Fisheries. In many countries, including the USA, rabies vaccine is given as part of a puppy's primary vaccination.

Below: *To cover the major canine diseases, inoculations should be given at 12 weeks with annual boosters after that*

Annual boosters are always recommended by vets and vaccine manufacturers. They are certainly advisable for the first 3 or 4 years but it is doubtful whether they are strictly necessary thereafter, though boarding kennels will insist on up-to-date boosters in order to protect themselves.

TEETHING

The puppy develops its milk teeth at about five weeks of age (these are the sharp needles that can cause you so much suffering if you have a boisterous, happy puppy!). They will drop out at four to eight months as the second teeth come through. Puppies will often swallow the milk teeth but this is not a cause for concern.

As the second teeth are coming through the puppy will need something to gnaw on, so you should provide a fresh knuckle bone or beef-hide dog chew for this purpose. You will also need to discourage him from using the table legs or other furniture instead!

SOCIALIZING

When you take your puppy home at 8-12 weeks of age he will probably be loving to everyone, as he will have no preconceived ideas of who is friend or stranger. You want your dog to grow up to accept everyone you invite into your house, so encourage him to be friendly to your visitors and, in turn, encourage them to treat him as another member of the family. This is essential, because he must learn that people other than members of the family are welcome.

Instil in him the idea that it is his house and that uninvited strangers should not be allowed in. He will begin to show the required

Below: 'Kurt' demonstrates hand-holding; one of the ways in which a Dobermann will display its pleasure

guarding instinct anywhere from five to ten months of age and you can encourage him to develop this by telling him to 'go and see who's there.' By using the correct tone of voice, you can create a feeling of unease which will put him on his guard. He will soon catch on and before long he will bark when anyone comes to the gate or door.

He must also learn to stop barking once you are aware of the impending 'danger', particularly if it is a false alarm. Barking can become a bad habit if not checked.

While puppies should not be left alone for long periods, your dog should learn to be alone for reasonable lengths of time without becoming upset. You can teach him to accept this very easily by leaving him alone in one room of the house (preferably the room with his bed in it) and telling to to 'stay, good boy, stay'. Leave him for a few minutes, keeping within hearing range. Tell him 'be quiet' if necessary. Return within a short while and praise him. Repeat at regular intervals, increasing the duration of the isolation.

When you do return home you will experience a Dobermann greeting, which is one of the breed's most endearing characteristics. This will vary from dog to dog but will include the bringing of presents (usually a cushion or a shoe), smiling, the clacking of teeth, hand-holding, or simply putting the front paws on your shoulders and demanding a cuddle. Do not mistake smiling and tooth-clacking as signs of aggression; those that do it will tend to use it as a means of communication, and are likely to do it increasingly as they get older, particularly if you give them any encouragement.

In getting your dog to accept your friends and family, you must make sure that children do not tease your dog, whatever his age, as this may encourage him to play rough or, even worse, to retaliate.

Once he has been inoculated at 12–14 weeks of age, you should begin to introduce him to the

Above: *An enthusiastic greeting like this one is characteristic of a Dobermann's desire for close physical contact with its owner.*

outside world. Get him used to going out on a collar and lead, but do not frighten him. Traffic can be terrifying to a small puppy. He will learn to accept it better if he is allowed to grow up with it as part of his background. If you live in a town, take him for short walks on the pavement, keeping him on your left-hand side (i.e. away from traffic), on a short lead and using plenty of voice and hand encouragement.

Show training (ringcraft) and obedience training classes are both excellent for socializing puppies as they help to get them used to people and other dogs.

A puppy will learn to accept cats, or indeed other animals, at an early age if they are part of his surroundings. However, he may well love your cat but still chase your neighbour's!

Your Dobermann may not have much contact with other animals such as cows, sheep and horses, but should always be taught not to chase them and if they are in the vicinity you should keep him on the lead.

LEAD TRAINING

This should start at an early age, ideally within a few days of the puppy arriving. Buy an inexpensive leather collar, large enough to allow for the first few months' growth (if necessary, punch a few additional holes in it to make it fit). Once he is fully grown, you can buy him a better quality collar — as a rough guide, you will need a 16 inch (41cm) collar for a bitch and 18 inch (45cm) for a dog.

Put the collar on him just to get him used to wearing it. This is likely to result in protests and attempts to remove it, but if you provide him with other distractions he will soon forget about it. Once the collar has been accepted, clip a lead on to it. More protests are likely, possibly quite vocal, once the implication of being on a lead is understood. Be gentle and don't frighten him. Keeping the lead short, talk to him, tickle him under the chin, pet him and coax him to walk by giving gentle jerks on the lead and praising him when he does walk. Stop frequently to give reassurance. Bribery often helps — cooked liver or cheese biscuits will usually provide an incentive to walk. Once he gets the general idea, try walking him round the lawn or garden. At first he will come with you in a series of leaps and jerks, but this uncertainty is soon overcome.

When he first goes out on to the road, don't overdo it. Don't let him be frightened by traffic and the rush of everyday life but give him time to absorb everything. As with any form of training, he will need plenty of encouragement and reassurance.

HOUSE TRAINING

If your puppy was bred in a kennel where he had free access to an outside run, he is likely to be largely house trained when you acquire him. Dobermanns are naturally clean and always prefer to go outside if possible.

House training a puppy is basically common sense. When he has eaten, put him outside. When he wakes up, put him outside. Tell him to 'go and be quick' and wait with him. He will soon learn why he has gone outside. Once he has obliged, praise him, then take him back into the house. In fine weather, leave your back door open so that he can go in and out as necessary.

A young puppy on three meals per day will need to go out at regular intervals, so you must always watch him and anticipate his needs. Equally, he will soon indicate when he wants to go out by going to the door and walking back and forth in obvious distress. If you get an occasional mishap, do not be too concerned as this must be expected. A mop and pail will come in handy, as will a roll of kitchen tissues. Restrict him to certain rooms until he is housetrained. This will reduce the risk of accidents all over the house.

Do not give him a drink late at night. Offer him one after his evening meal, then pick up the water until the morning. Put him outside again last thing before bed and he should be clean through the night. If you can let him out during the night, or at least first thing in the morning, he should soon learn to be clean through the night. Training puppies to use newspaper on the floor at night is often advocated, but is in reality counter-productive as it encourages them to think that indoor sanitation is acceptable. They should learn that this is never so.

If you have an adult dog that is not houseclean during the night, it may be because of your feeding schedule. Ensure that he is fed in the evening, not in the morning, does not have access to water during the night and goes outside last thing at night and first thing in the morning. As a last resort, chain the dog to his bed, making sure that the chain is sufficiently long so as not to cause him any discomfort. This often works because no dog will deliberately foul its own bed. If the problem persists, it may be a good idea to get your dog checked by a vet to ensure that it is not caused by a health problem.

INSURANCE

Many breeders will ensure that you have a one-month temporary insurance cover on your puppy when you buy him. This will enable you to recover the purchase price of your puppy (or his insured value, if different) in the event of his death or if he is lost or stolen. It will also give you limited cover against vet's fees as well as a few other additional benefits. Such policies are a very good idea, as the first month that the puppy is with you is the period of greatest risk as he faces a new home, new environment, change of food and water, and inoculations.

This temporary cover can be extended into a general pet policy, which will include third party insurance and vet's fees arising from any cause. It is up to you to decide whether to insure your Dobermann, but I would strongly advise you to take out third party cover if nothing else. This will not cost you very much per year and will give you cover in respect of legal liability for any damage done by your dog to other people or their property and for any legal costs incurred. It will not cover damage to your own property, but this can be provided for on your household insurance policy.

If you are self-employed or you can demonstrate a tangible link between your home and your work, it is more than likely that you will be able to claim tax relief on your guard dog. If you are eligible, you will be able to claim the purchase price of the dog and the essential costs of keeping him, such as feeding, vet's fees, insurance and any necessary equipment such as bedding, collars and leads.

ACCOMMODATION

The proper place for your Dobermann to live is in the house with his humans. The house will very quickly become his house which you share with him. As long

Below: *'Rita' shows off the ideal dog-bed for the home, though most Dobes prefer an armchair! This bed is lined with carpet.*

as you realise this simple fact from the outset, there will be no problems later. The Dobermann is a very affectionate dog who always wants to be close to his family. His being a house dog will enable you and him to develop that close bond of love, loyalty and trust that is such an essential part of your relationship. It will also enable you to develop his personality and character, teach him everything he needs to know, socialize him, encourage him to guard the house and, most important of all, you will enjoy the unique pleasure and satisfaction of having a Dobermann in the house with you.

Your Dobermann's desire to be with you is, in reality, an extension of the 'pack animal' characteristic of all dogs. You are accepted as the pack leader and he is part of the pack, so he wants to be in close contact with you at all times. A dog which loses this contact and is left outside alone in a kennel becomes isolated and can very easily develop an abnormal temperament and personality problems.

BEDDING

The choice of bed will depend to some extent on whether your Dobermann is to live in the house or in a kennel. If he is to live in the house, which I hope he will, you should provide him with a small box with high sides to prevent draughts. Wood is ideal, as it is long-lasting and can be scrubbed clean when necessary, although less durable materials may be used for a small puppy on the basis that the bed is only going to last for a short time. It should be located somewhere which is warm and away from draughts, and this will be his sanctuary to which he can retire whenever he feels the need. Make it comfortable, so that it is attractive to him — an old blanket is ideal, but he should be discouraged from chewing it.

If the puppy has a wooden box, make sure that the front is low enough to allow him to get in and out easily and safely. Avoid wicker

baskets, as they are easily chewed, which is bad for the basket, and bad for your puppy or dog if he swallows bits of the wicker.

There are a wide variety of dog beds which you can buy. These include plastic beds, which can be cold and austere, although many Dobermanns appear to accept them happily. Bean bags are generally popular with Dobermanns, and may even be carried around the house by them.

Dobermanns also love fires. They will sit as close to one as they can and stay there until the heat becomes unbearable. This will not hurt your dog, but do take the same basic precautions as you would for a child — always put a guard in front of the fire if you leave it unattended.

The kennel

If you propose to make your dog sleep in an outside kennel you should ensure that it is windproof and watertight and that he has an enclosed wooden box inside it. It is a good idea for the kennel door to have a trapdoor, hinged at the top, set in it, so that he can get out, either to the garden or into an enclosed run. This will keep the kennel clean, leaving you only the outside run to clear out.

The kennel should be heated, as the Dobermann has a short coat and so feels the cold. The safest and most convenient means of heating is an infra-red electric wall heater, fitted with a thermostat. Do not use paraffin or gas heaters, as they can give off harmful fumes and may also be knocked over and possibly start a fire. Make sure that the wall heater is out of the dog's reach and that it is mounted on a sheet of asbestos, if the building is a wooden one, in order to reduce any fire risk. During the winter period, you should aim to maintain a temperature of about 45–50°F (7–10°C) in the kennel.

The box for an adult Dobermann will need to be about 3ft 6 inch (1.6m) wide, 2ft 6inches (76cm) deep and 3ft 6inches (1.6m) high. A fully enclosed box is better as it will

give added warmth. The front can be open, with a 6 inch (15cm) high horizontal sliding board. This will enable your Dobermann to get in and out, while at the same time shielding him from draughts and keeping the bedding in the box. The box should be raised off the ground by up to 6 inches (15cm). This will prevent dampness and allow ventilation.

Straw and paper

For bedding, provide a piece of carpet with a blanket on top or straw. Barley straw is the softest and most comfortable, while wheat straw is harder so does not break down so quickly and is less likely to harbour pests. There is always a risk that straw will contain fleas, but this is not likely to be a problem under normal circumstances. Keep any stock of straw dry and clean and keep vermin away from it — and this includes cats! Change the straw bedding whenever it breaks down or becomes dirty; old straw can be spread on the garden, composted or burnt.

Shredded paper is also a satisfactory bedding material, provided you acquire soft, clean paper. It is easy to dispose of but does tend to blow around everywhere and, unlike straw, does not break down and rot away. The important thing is that your Dobermann is kept warm and dry.

Above: A bed for an outside kennel, built of wood for easy cleaning. Note the sliding board to hold in the straw bedding.

Not only will this ensure that he is comfortable and happy but it will reduce the likelihood of him becoming ill. It will also mean that he is not using his energy just to keep warm.

The floor

Sawdust is the ideal material for a kennel floor and will keep the kennel dry. It is easily obtained and is usually inexpensive and often free. Fouled sawdust should be picked up as and when necessary and disposed of by being composted, burnt or removed from the premises in bags.

The use of disinfectant in water in the kennel each day is not to be recommended, as this makes the kennel damp; it is far better to wash out the kennel properly when necessary, preferably during the warmer summer months. Use hot water with added detergent, washing soda and some disinfectant. This is an ideal brew as the detergent will dissolve the grease and dirt and the soda will kill most, if not all, germs. There are a number of disinfectants on the market which claim to kill all known germs including parvovirus and there is no reason why you should not use one of these if you wish to as an aid to preventing disease.

Clean the wooden bed as well, using a standard wooden scrubbing-brush, and wash any blankets regularly. Ensure that the bed and bedding are fully dry before the dog uses them again.

EXERCISE

While he is still a small puppy your Dobermann will not require any specific exercise — he will get all he needs running around the house and playing in the garden. If the weather is cold, do not let him stay outside too long; it is very important to keep him warm and dry if he is to stay healthy. While your puppy may seem big and strong he is, in reality, a very delicate animal who needs careful watching.

Dobermanns hate rain and in wet weather your dog is quite likely to demand re-entry to the house very soon after going out. Do not make him stay out in the rain longer than necessary, as the Dobermann's fine, short coat allows him to get wet very quickly. If he comes in wet, rub him down with an old towel or with crumpled newspaper.

Exercise is not needed until your Dobermann is about four months old, and, up to eight months, it should be limited. Never attempt to go too far — little and often is the best adage. Between four and eight months of age, the bones of your Dobermann will be very largely cartilage. As the puppy grows, this cartilage is replaced by bone and, until this happens, over-exercise could cause the front legs to bend and the pasterns to soften.

Keeping fit
Once your puppy reaches eight months old, you are reasonably safe in increasing the amount of exercise he gets. Even so, the notion that a Dobermann needs miles and miles of walking each day is a fallacy. Your Dobermann will keep fit with relatively small amounts of exercise, the main benefit of which is for him to explore other territory and to see who has

Below: *Running free in its own run is generally sufficient to keep a Dobermann fit and regularly exercised.*

been in the area. It is therefore very largely a mental and psychological need that is being met rather than a physical one. The exercise is also likely to be of some benefit to you!

Ideally, the exercise should strike a balance between controlled road walking on the lead and free running. Road walking will help to harden up the muscles, strengthen the body and give the dog that hard, strong, muscular appearance which is such an important part of the Dobermann's physiology.

Exercise must be balanced with feeding — too much exercise will give you a super-fit, but also a thin dog. A Dobermann should carry a reasonable amount of substance and his bones should certainly not show. For a dog which has unrestricted freedom of the house and garden, half an hour's exercise morning and evening would be a reasonable estimate. Always arrange to take him out before his meal, not after it; it is dangerous to let him take violent exercise on a full stomach as this is a frequent cause of bloat (gastric tortion).

Aggression

Once your Dobermann reaches about ten months old his true character will be developing. Any dog which shows belligerence towards him is likely to get a sharp response. Always remember that a Dobermann, particularly a male, is likely to have a fight with another male of almost any breed. Dog fights can be very unpleasant and difficult to break up. They are also likely to result in damage to your dog and even to you. The moral is simple — don't let your dog off the lead unless you are quite sure that it is safe to do so, and never let him off the lead anywhere until you are quite satisfied that he has learned to come when he is called or to sit and stay on command. In this way you will at least have some control over your dog.

BONES AND STONES

A fresh knuckle bone is excellent for keeping a young puppy occupied and giving him something on which to chew when teething. Apart from when he is a young puppy, however, you should *never* give your dog a bone to chew. An adult Dobermann has a very powerful set of jaws and can crunch considerable amounts off a bone in a relatively short space of time; this is the direct cause of many Dobermanns (and other breeds) having to undergo operations each year or even losing their lives. The dog may swallow a considerable amount of bone chippings from, say, a marrow bone, which then get impacted in the intestine. There is always the risk that one of these may puncture the intestine, resulting in peritonitis and possibly septicaemia.

If you must give him a bone, make sure that it is one he cannot chew too much off — shank bone is probably safest. Never give your dog cooked bones of any sort; these become brittle and are more liable to splinter. Chicken and rabbit bones are particularly dangerous. If you want to provide your dog with something on which to gnaw, it is much better to give him a beef-hide chew. These are to be found in pet shops and supermarkets and come in various sizes; they will give hours of pleasure and will not do any harm, since any pieces swallowed will be digested.

Dobermann puppies are invariably fascinated with stones, and will often carry them around and play with them. This is a habit which should be discouraged, as there is always a risk that one might be swallowed and if it cannot be passed through the system an operation will be necessary.

If your puppy appears off-colour for no apparent reason, is losing body and is not eating or producing motions, a swallowed stone (or other item) may be the cause. Ask your vet to carry out an X-ray to check this possibility. Apart from stones, knobs off cupboard doors and everyday household items, such as nylon pot-scrapers, have been known to be responsible. The latter can badly lacerate the intestines and do not show up on an X-ray plate. The moral here is simple — keep everything out of your puppy's reach. There is nothing like having a Dobermann puppy in the house for teaching you to be tidy!

TOYS

It is a good idea to give your puppy toys to play with as they will keep him occupied, possibly for hours at a time, and adult Dobermanns enjoy them too. Do not give him anything he can swallow or injure himself on. Never give a puppy an old slipper or shoe to play with. This will teach him to chew shoes and he will never be able to distinguish your new shoes from your old ones.

Rubber rings and rubber balls are ideal, as long as the balls are sufficiently large for him not be able to swallow them or get them stuck in the back of his throat. Older dogs will also like them, but many adult Dobermanns will promptly chew a rubber ring into little pieces. If your dog is a destroyer, such toys are clearly of no use, as not only are they a waste of money but he might swallow bits of rubber.

Dobermanns will invariably find their own toys, such as lumps of

mud, bits of wood, logs and lengths of hosepipe. Any toy such as this is all right, but always watch in case he gets into trouble, such as getting a bit of stick stuck across the roof of his mouth — not an uncommon occurrence.

When you play with your puppy, do not do it in such a way as to encourage him to become rough. Never allow him to bite or to have mock battles. You want him to play gently, as there is nothing worse than a full-sized Dobermann who wants to have rough games.

Apart from keeping a lively and active young Dobermann occupied, toys can be used as an aid to training. Most of the basic obedience exercises can be taught at home with toys or titbits without the puppy realizing that he is being trained.

CAR SICKNESS

Most puppies are sick when they first travel in a car or, if not actually sick, they frequently salivate. It is almost certain that your puppy will

Below: *The natural beauty of a Dobermann's coat can be enhanced by grooming with either a grooming glove or soft brush.*

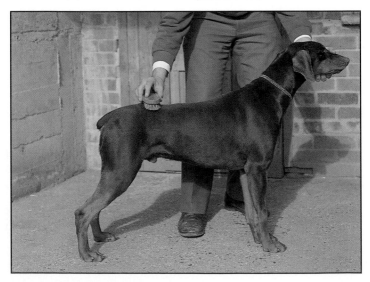

grow out of this, but you will need to get him used to the car at an early age. If you do not, you may always have a dog who is unhappy in cars. The simplest way is to take him out for short journeys, always on an empty stomach. He will gradually begin to take an interest in everything around him and drool less. If the journeys have specific objectives such as a walk in the park or a training class he will associate the car with something pleasant, thereby helping him to forget his discomfort.

It may help to give him something to occupy his mind during these early journeys, such as a beef-hide chew. I am not in favour of travel-sickness pills, as these only partially relieve the symptoms without curing the cause. It is far better to take him out little and often, putting plenty of newspaper under him to catch any flow and mopping up as necessary with paper towels. This is simply one of those little problems which you must overcome.

Once he has learnt to accept the car, he will almost certainly enjoy being in it. It will very soon become an extension of his home, which he will guard instinctively — and of course, anything in it. It is a very brave man, or a very stupid one, who would break into a car with an adult Dobermann in it. Even so, with younger animals be extra careful; it is not unknown for Dobermann puppies to be stolen from inside cars.

GROOMING

A fit and healthy Dobermann, fed on a correct diet, will exhibit that smooth shining coat that is so typical of the breed. This appearance cannot be created by grooming alone, though it can help to enhance it. For this breed, grooming needs are minimal. Use either a soft hand-brush or a hound-glove and gently brush the coat in the same direction as the lie of hair, i.e. from head towards tail. Your dog will enjoy this. Dobermanns moult or shed twice a year, as do most breeds. You will rarely see the hair that is shed, however, as it is very fine in texture. You should only need to groom your Dobermann for a few minutes at a time and about twice per week. Grooming routines such as stripping and trimming are not necessary.

There is little need for any surface dressing to be applied, though this is generally done as part of the preparation for the show-ring. If you want to add a coat-dressing, liquid paraffin or any proprietary brand of hair conditioner can be used. Massage it into the coat, again working with the lie of it.

Below: *Your Dobermann can be best cared for with such equipment as nail-clippers, tooth scraper, soft brush and cotton wool.*

BATHING

Under normal circumstances your
Dobermann will only need the
occasional bath, possibly once per
year. Bathing more frequently is not
necessary and may remove the
natural oils, leaving him with a dry,
harsh coat. By choice, bathing is
best done in warm, sunny weather
when the coat will dry quickly. In
cold weather you can use a hair-
dryer; although most Dobermanns
dislike them until they get used to
them.

Bathing should always be done in
warm, shallow water, say up to 12
inches (30cm) in depth. Persuading
your Dobermann to get into the
bath can be a problem, but the
easiest way is to stand him
alongside the bath, swing his back
end in first, then swing his front
end in. Allow him to remain
standing up. Use a proprietary
brand of dog shampoo, which
should be diluted with water in an
old jug, then gently poured over the
coat and massaged in by hand.
Using the same jug, pour water
from the bath over his coat to wash
out the soap, being careful not to
get any shampoo in his eyes.

Eyes

It is normal for a grey mucus
discharge to collect in the corners
of the eyes. Use a small cotton
wool swab and, gently holding the
dog's head with one hand, wipe
away from the eye, not across it.
This should be done each morning
and at other times as necessary; it
is one of those routine operations
that you will soon perfect and your
dog will accept.

If the mucus becomes thick and
yellow-green in colour, this
indicates the presence of some
infection. Ask your vet for a tube of
eye ointment and squeeze a small
amount into the affected eye. This
should clear the infection very
quickly, but if the dog is in obvious
discomfort or you are worried that
the problem is more serious, take
him to your vet.

Ears

Check your dog's ears at regular
intervals. It is quite normal for a
black, waxy substance to collect
there which, if not removed, may
well cause irritation or infection.

Clean the ears once every two
weeks taking great care not to hurt
the dog, as this is a very sensitive
area. Make sure that you have a
good source of light so that you
can really see what you are doing.
The best way to do this is with a
cotton wool swab held firmly in a
pair of artery forceps. Dip the swab
in methylated spirits and squeeze it
between your fingers to remove
most of the surplus fluid, then work
it gently around the inside of the
ear. The methylated spirits will
loosen the wax, enabling it to be
removed easily on the swab.

It is not a good idea to use water
as inevitably some will remain inside
the ears and may be the source of
problems. You should also avoid
using oily substances, as any
residue left in the ears can act as a
culture medium and encourage the
growth of ear mites.

If the inside of the ears are red
and appear sore, ask your vet for a
tube of ear ointment or some ear
drops. Squeeze a small amount into
the ear and smear it gently around
the inside. You may find ear mites
in the course of cleaning the ears;
they look like fine sand-like granules

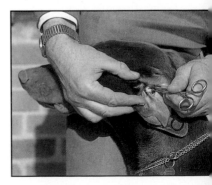

Right: *Ears should be cleaned
regularly. Use cotton wool clamped
in artery forceps and dipped in
methylated spirits.*

on the swabs and there will also be an unpleasant smell in the ears. The methylated spirits will help to clear them, as will drops or ointment. Ear mites should be dealt with as quickly as possible, as they can cause intense irritation and, eventually, permanent damage to the ears. If your dog repeatedly scratches his ears, check to see if this is the reason.

Teeth

You should clean your dog's teeth regularly in order to reduce the risk of dental decay and gum problems. Start while he is still a puppy, so that he learns to accept it. He will certainly not like it, so you will have to use your powers of persuasion and at the same time try not to upset him too much.

Cleaning involves removing the yellow discoloration off of the teeth and is best done with a cotton wool swab, dipped in a solution of sodium bicarbonate. If the stain is particularly bad, as it may be with an older dog whose teeth have been neglected, it may be necessary to use something stronger; a smokers' toothpaste is very effective! Many Dobermanns develop a passion for peppermint toothpaste, so this may be worth trying first.

You will also need to remove any scale from the teeth. This is a hard, chalky deposit which builds up, particularly on the molars, and is caused by the secretion from the salivary glands. Ideally, a tooth scaler should be used for this purpose but the pointed end of a nail file will suffice. Whatever you use you will need to exercise great care, as you may need to exert quite strong pressure in order to chip the scale off the teeth. Always work away from the gums during this routine, so as to avoid the risk of hurting them.

Scaling a dog's teeth is something which owners frequently leave for the experts, such as the vet or professional dog groomers, to do for them. However, it is not difficult and you should learn to do it for yourself.

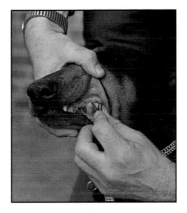

Above: *Teeth scale should not be allowed to build up. Use a metal scaler on a regular basis to help keep teeth clean.*

Nails

Your dog's nails should be kept short in order to avoid discomfort and possible damage to the feet. If your Dobermann has good feet the nails will remain relatively short and need little or no attention, but in the case of many dogs they will require regular clipping. Cut them back with either a pair of nail clippers or a guillotine-type cutter. Always make sure that you know where the quick is — it is better to err on the side of caution and take off too little rather than risk cutting the quick as this will hurt the dog, and he will be less willing to trust you. If you do inadvertently cut the quick, the bleeding can be stopped by the application of potassium permanganate crystals. If you use nail clippers the nails should be nicked on each side before being cut, as there is a risk of splitting a nail if you attempt to cut through it in one operation. You may find that in fact it is easier to clip off the end of the nails and then file them back with a coarse wood file.

Few dogs enjoy having their nails cut and many positively object. You should therefore get them used to it from an early age. If you are uneasy about doing it yourself, seek assistance from your vet, a dog parlour or an experienced breeder.

THE DOG

Young dogs become aware of their sexuality from about nine months of age. This is merely part of the normal growing up process and is rarely a problem in a kennel where a young dog is generally placed with an older bitch who will generally put him in his place very quickly. Even in the house adolescent sexual adventures are not a serious problem, merely one that can be embarrassing at times. Do not make a major issue out of it; give him a firm command, 'no'. Your dog will soon learn that these 'experiments' are not acceptable. However, you should avoid inhibiting him too much as a puppy if you are planning a stud career for him in the future.

Regrettably, some vets advocate castration as the cure for this sex play. While this will remove the ability to reproduce it does not prevent the sexual urge, or indeed the ability to mate a bitch. Castration is also often put forward as the cure for aggressiveness in the adult dog, but a naturally aggressive dog will be just as aggressive after being castrated as before. Castrating young dogs is wrong, because the sexual hormones are an essential part of the growing up process. Even with an adult dog, castration should not be done unless there are good reasons and certainly not before two years of age.

Monorchids

A dog which has only one testicle is generally known as a monorchid. Technically, this term is incorrect, as most such dogs are really unilateral cryptorchids, in that one testicle has been retained in the abdomen instead of descending into the scrotum as it should. Retained testicles have a tendency to become cancerous and ideally should be surgically removed, but again only after the dog is mature.

Injections of testosterone can be given at about four months of age to try to bring down a retained testicle, but this is not normally successful. In any event, the use of hormones should be avoided as far as possible as they may have undesirable side effects. Since it is a hereditary factor affecting the fertility of the dog, you should avoid using a monorchid dog at stud. Occasionally both testicles will be retained in the abdomen. Such a dog is known as a bilateral cryptorchid, and will be infertile.

THE BITCH

Most bitches come into season twice a year at approximately six-monthly intervals, (see Section II for more details). You should keep a record of the dates that your bitch comes into season, so that you will always know roughly when her next one is due.

When your bitch is in season you will need to keep her well away from visiting dogs in order to avoid an unwanted litter, even if it means restricting her daily exercise. Remember that she may be trying to get out to find herself a dog and keep a close eye on her movements.

The onset of a season often induces changes of temperament. Puppies may become nervous and edgy, but this will generally pass as the season wanes. Older bitches may become excitable and it is not uncommon for them to mount other bitches. This does no apparent harm, so long as the second bitch is reasonably tolerant. If necessary, gentle persuasion will generally stop it.

Do not breed from your bitch until she is two years old or more. While she may be physically capable of producing puppies at an earlier age, she will not be sufficiently developed physically or mentally. She herself will be prevented from developing fully and will not have sufficient maturity and body adequately to produce and rear the puppies; consequently the puppies themselves are likely to be smaller and inferior in quality.

As a general rule, if a bitch has reared a litter of puppies she should not be mated at the following season. Possible exceptions to this may be where the litter was small, say three puppies or less, or all the puppies died at birth. Leaving a period of at least one year between successive litters will allow the bitch to reach peak condition again.

No bitch should be mated once she has reached seven years of age as there is a real risk of whelping problems. It is also unwise to breed from a maiden bitch once she is five years of age or more for the same reason.

Irrespective of age or previous breeding record, no bitch should be used for breeding if she is not in peak physical condition. Many brood bitches become fat and flabby by six years of age and should not be used for breeding, as the lack of muscle tone is again likely to lead to whelping problems.

Do not resort to hormone injections designed to stop a bitch from coming into season. While these sound ideal in theory, in practice they often disrupt the normal cycle, resulting in the bitch coming into season at unpredictable times. They also

frequently have the undesirable side effect of preventing the bitch from conceiving at subsequent seasons. As a general rule, you should avoid the use of any hormone treatments unless they are absolutely necessary.

False pregnancies
The majority of Dobermann bitches have false pregnancies after each season. This is because the bitch has a higher than normal level of progesterone, whether or not she has been mated. The symptoms are normally slight, with the bitch merely showing an enlargement of the teats, the formation of milk and a tendency to gain weight. These symptoms reach their peak some nine weeks after the season, i.e. when the litter would have been born had she been mated. The best remedy for this particular problem is to do nothing and allow the course of nature to solve it.

Below: *Before you even consider breeding from your bitch, you must make sure that she is mature enough and in the best condition.*

Reducing the fluid intake, cutting down the carbohydrate content of the food and increasing the exercise may help.

Having a false pregnancy does not mean a bitch wants or needs a litter of puppies, nor can it be cured by allowing the bitch to have a litter — she will still have a false pregnancy at the next season. Occasionally a bitch will suffer mental symptoms as well, collecting up her toys as substitute puppies and becoming broody. Do not encourage these symptoms in any way; ignore them, and again the situation will resolve itself naturally. However, if this problem continually causes unacceptable domestic nuisance, it may be worth considering having the bitch spayed.

A phantom pregnancy is similar to a false pregnancy but occurs where the bitch has been mated and shows all the expected signs of having a litter when she has not, in fact, conceived.

Spaying

If you must spay your bitch for purely social reasons, you should not do so until she is at least 18 months of age. As with the males, the sex hormones produced by the bitch are necessary for her normal development. Spaying should be done midway between two seasons, when the blood supply to the reproductive organs is at its minimum. Spayed bitches often develop a slight but constant leak from the vulva. This is not easily resolved and is one of the adverse side effects of spaying. It can also be very difficult to prevent spayed bitches from becoming obese.

THE VETERAN

Your Dobermann will officially become a veteran once he reaches seven years of age. There is nothing magical about this threshold, but it should make you realize that he is becoming an old dog. The life expectation of a Dobermann is generally reckoned to be between 8 and 12 years,

with ten being a good average, and there are a number of things that you can do to try to increase his chances of a longer life.

Bitches tend to put on weight as they become older, particularly if they have had litters, while dogs tend to retain their figures much better and to remain super-fit. An older dog may appear to be healthy and capable of taking unlimited exercise, but you must think for him; only allow limited, controlled exercise so as to reduce the strain on the heart. This is particularly important with males, who often suffer from heart failure when in apparently perfect health.

Do not overfeed and, if necessary, reduce the quantity of food in order to prevent him from putting on too much weight. Obesity is likely to result in the dog taking too little exercise and extra strain being put on the heart.

Older dogs often have difficulty in digesting one large meal each day. This may manifest itself by the dog appearing to be tucked-up and uncomfortable after eating, being unwilling to eat all his food, suffering from bloat or vomiting soon after eating. You can help by giving the meal in two halves, one in the morning and the other in the evening, thereby reducing the pressure on the stomach. Drinking excessive quantities of water, sometimes sufficient to cause bloat, may also be a problem, in which case you must control the fluid intake. Drinking abnormally large amounts can be due to diabetes or to a kidney problem, so arrange for a urine test to be carried out by your veterinarian.

Bitches often develop mammary tumours or other lumps on their undersides. If these grow rapidly or cause problems it may be advisable to have them surgically removed; usually they are benign and grow relatively slowly so are best left alone. If they are excised others seem to develop quite quickly and the anaesthetic and the shock of the operation sometimes kill the bitch. In any case, it is often kinder to accept that these tumours may

eventually end the bitch's life rather than put her through the pain and suffering of an operation which may do little to extend it.

Older dogs sometimes lose complete control of their bowels or bladders. This is generally a progressive problem which causes as much distress to the dog as to its owner. There is little that can be done to overcome this as it is part of the ageing process, though it can be controlled to some extent by encouraging the dog to go out to relieve himself more frequently.

Some dogs gradually lose the co-ordination in their hind legs. This is generally quite slight initially but can get progressively worse until, in extreme cases, the dog is unable to get up unaided. This is simply a degenerative process due to ageing and should not be confused with disease.

Other faculties such as hearing and sight may also deteriorate. Loss of hearing is not likely to cause many problems, though you should avoid any unseen approach which may startle the dog. Loss of sight rarely seems to cause dogs any undue concern and they adapt remarkably well. Ensure that objects are not left on pathways and try to retain familiar room layouts as the dog will rely on his memory as much as his sight.

The older dog will feel the cold more, so be prepared to keep his environment warmer when necessary. He will also tend to sleep more than when he was younger and should be allowed to rest as much as he needs.

The day may come when you have to make the difficult decision as to whether to allow your Dobermann to continue living or if it is kinder to put him to sleep. This decision needs to be the result of a balanced judgement. Do not act with unseemly haste and betray him when he needs you most in his final days simply because he is old, tatty or losing his faculties. Allow him to continue for as long as he is able to eat, take exercise and derive some pleasure from his life. Only when he is clearly in pain or is unable to lead anything approaching a normal life should you allow him to die in peace and with dignity. The best way to overcome your grief at losing your Dobermann, whatever his age, is to acquire another one as soon as possible. The new dog can never replace the old one but he will fill the gap.

Chapter Four

HEALTH CARE

By nature, the Dobermann is normally a very fit and healthy dog. As with any animal, however, there may be times when he is sick and needs treatment. Your task is to learn to distinguish the routine problems which you can treat at home from the more serious ones which will require veterinary attention. This is very largely a matter of common sense and experience. If you are ever in doubt, however, it is always wise to be cautious and visit your vet. This will ensure that proper treatment is received as early as possible.

POTENTIAL BREED PROBLEMS

In the following sections I have described some of the ailments that you are more likely to encounter as they specifically affect Dobermanns. There are many other health problems that may affect your dog, but if in doubt do consult your veterinary surgeon.

Hip Dysplasia (HD)
The hip is essentially a ball and socket joint, with the ball (the femoral head) fitting tightly into the socket (the acetabulum of the pelvis). In dogs with HD, the ball does not fit the acetabulum. There may also be some associated breakdown of the two bones. This defect is considered to be multifactorial with an hereditary component. Environmental factors

also play a large part. HD can cause pain and lameness to affected dogs, the extent of which is dependent upon the severity of the defect.

HD is not a serious breed problem, but does occur occasionally. The state of the hips can only be determined by the expert analysis of X-rays. If you are concerned about your dog's hips you should ask your vet to do an X-ray and send it for expert orthopaedic evaluation. Any dog showing a considerable deviation from the norm should not be used for breeding, though there is no reason why it should not live a normal life in every other way. Only where the dog's hips are extremely defective is he likely to have weak hind movement or impaired mobility and this does not happen often in the breed due to Hip Dysplasia.

You can minimize the chances of your dog suffering from HD by not over-exercising him as a puppy, when his bones are soft and cartilagenous and can be easily damaged. The bones have generally hardened sufficiently by nine months to allow unrestricted exercise. HD can also be induced by overfeeding growing puppies, particularly with high levels of protein or over-nutritious food, since this leads to faulty development of cartilage and this causes problems in the change-over from cartilage to bone. Also do not allow your puppy to put on excess weight.

Cervical Spondylopathy (CS)

CS is caused by deformities within the seven cervical (neck) vertebrae. If these vertebrae are malformed or move too freely one against another, the spinal cord which runs through the vertebrae comes under pressure, thereby affecting the dog's ability to move. In addition, the discs between the vertebrae may be affected and their contents squeezed into the canal, so reducing its size and putting additional pressure on the spinal cord.

Research has indicated that the problem usually occurs at the base of the neck and that nearly 80 per cent of Dobermanns X-rayed have some degree of deviation from the norm, though the number of Dobermanns actually showing any physical symptoms is a very small percentage of the total breed population. These symptoms are uncoordinated movement and clumsy, awkward steps, which have led to this problem also being called the 'wobbler syndrome' and affected dogs 'wobblers'. Hind leg weakness is often a sign and should not be confused with Hip Dysplasia.

The cause of CS is not really known but there is no evidence to indicate that it is due to a hereditary component, though breed conformation may be a contributory factor. Overfeeding or feeding an over nutritious diet could increase the incidence of CS, due to the resultant increase in the growth rate. In addition, damage to the neck vertebrae may be caused by external factors such as accidental damage to the neck or the improper use of a choke-chain. Even the weight of the head has been implicated by some authors!

X-ray examination of your Dobermann's neck will certainly tell you whether it is normal or to what extent it deviates. If your dog has a serious abnormality and is at risk of becoming a wobbler it would not be prudent to use him for breeding, although it is to be hoped that further research will give some guidance as to what causes the initial deformity, whether it is hereditary and how to avoid a dog with CS becoming a wobbler. Once these questions have been answered it should be possible to give advice to Dobermann owners and breeders as to how to interpret their dogs' X-rays and eventually reduce or even eliminate this problem.

Below: *Taking the heart beat of a patient. Inevitably, there will be occasions when you will need the help and advice of a vet.*

Eye problems

Dobermanns on the whole suffer few eye problems. Progressive Retinal Atrophy, which causes hereditary blindness, is not a problem in the breed although an hereditary condition affecting the back of the lens and the adjacent vitreous body in the eye has been reported in several European countries and the United States.

The eye should be almond shaped and deep set but if this is exaggerated at all problems of in-turning of the lids, or entropion, can occasionally be encountered. This can cause soreness and a runny eye or eyes. If in doubt seek veterinary advice.

PARASITIC PROBLEMS

Fleas

Fleas may occur at any time, but are generally more of a problem in hot, dry summer weather. The flea lays eggs away from the dog, usually in the bedding. These hatch, pass through a larval stage and turn into adult fleas ready to reinfect the dog. They suck blood and cause considerable irritation and scratching, which results in sore, bare patches. Strangely, some Dobermanns can be heavily infested and show few signs while others will show a hypersensitive reaction and scratch themselves to distraction over one flea.

Fleas act as intermediate hosts for a common canine tapeworm, which is a further reason for eliminating them. They are best removed by using aerosol sprays or dusting powder. Treat the dog's living quarters as well in order to kill or remove the egg and larval stages. You can buy flea collars but these should be used with caution as they give off a chemical vapour. Heavy infestations can be treated with an insecticidal dog shampoo.

Check for the presence of fleas with a fine-toothed metal comb, particularly in the summer.

Lice

Lice are light-brown insects longer than fleas and do not move as fast. They feed on the skin. Their eggs (nits) stick to the hair, generally around the neck and ears. Lice cannot live away from the dog for more than a few days and infection is spread from dog to dog by physical contact. The presence of lice causes great irritation and thus frequent scratching by the dog. Eliminate them by regular spraying with an insecticide.

Ticks

Ticks are not a common problem but dogs may occasionally pick them up, particularly in areas where sheep are found. They attach themselves to the dog's skin, and look like brown warts. Do not

Above: *As a breed, Dobermanns do not suffer from hereditary eye problems. Occasionally, however, they may contract eye infections.*

simply pull them off, as this will leave the head part buried in the skin and may cause an abscess. Ticks can be anaesthetized by applying surgical spirit or ether and can then be pulled gently until they release their hold.

Sarcoptic mange

This is caused by a microscopic mange mite which can usually be diagnosed from a skin scraping by the vet. The mites burrow into the surface layer of the skin. The first symptoms are usually small reddened bumps on the skin and persistent scratching. The skin becomes roughened with bare patches and hair loss.

Mange generally starts around the edges of the ears and eyes and on the legs but if not cured it will spread over the whole body. Veterinary advice should always be sought. Treatment should include bathing with an insecticidal shampoo which is specifically active against the mites. Three or four applications are normally adequate. Antibiotics may be supplied for the sore areas; the dog's sleeping area should also be treated with an insecticidal spray. An infected dog should be isolated, as sarcoptic mange is highly contagious.

Cheyletiella Mite infestation

This is commonly referred to as 'walking dandruff' and normally affects puppies. It is caused by a small mite which is invisible to the naked eye. It can be recognized by a heavy dandruff on the head, neck and back. As it causes some irritation, affected puppies are likely to scratch. Treatment should be similar to that for sarcoptic mange, but veterinary advice is worthwhile to establish the diagnosis.

Demodectic Mange

Also known as follicular or 'red' mange, this is caused by the Follicular mite (*Demodex canis*), which is present in the hair follicles of many dogs without causing any symptoms. The mites are passed from a bitch to her puppies during the first few weeks of their lives. A skin scraping from any dog is thus likely to reveal the presence of Demodex. On a few dogs the mites multiply rapidly and small bare patches appear round the eyes, nose, legs and feet. These sometimes cause no irritation to the dog. The first signs usually occur between three and 12 months of age and often clear up very quickly. Diagnosis by your vet is confirmed by skin scraping. Baths and dressing will probably be supplied to control it and the chances of cure today are much greater than formerly.

Occasionally the problem does not improve but gets worse, due to an immune deficiency.

Susceptibility to demodectic mange is not known but is almost certainly an inherited tendency, whereby certain dogs lack the necessary immunity. It is not transmitted by the sire, though he may transmit the tendency. As it depends on the dog's inherited lack of resistance, it is not highly contagious. Affected dogs should not be used for breeding.

Harvest Mites

It is the larval stage of the harvest mite which is parasitic and is usually found in the autumn, hence the name. The larvae look like orange-red pinheads, only just visible to the naked eye, and are usually found between the toes. They cause irritation, so that the dog will continually lick and nibble his feet. Harvest mites can be controlled by swabbing with methylated spirits or surgical spirit or by bathing with an insecticidal shampoo.

Ringworm

Ringworm is not caused by a worm, as its name might suggest but by a fungus which attacks the hair. It is transmitted by contact with other animals or with the spores of the fungus. It grows in circular bare patches, in man, but in the dog the skin is often crusty and thickened, and may be mistaken for the early stages of demodectic mange. Ringworm is diagnosed by skin scrapings. An infected dog should be isolated so as to avoid ringworm spreading. Special drugs and baths will be supplied by your veterinary surgeon.

ROUTINE PROBLEMS

Diarrhoea

This is one of the commonest problems that you are likely to encounter. It is the result of an upset bowel and is generally easy to cure. It is usually caused by something that has been eaten — usually too much fat, liver or milk or some other inappropriate food. Such diarrhoea is likely to resolve itself quickly, once the cause has been eliminated from the system.

You can help to prevent diarrhoea by avoiding feeding excessive raw milk, raw meat or dry biscuit meal as they can all upset the lining of the stomach and intestines. Make sure that the dinner is properly soaked. You can help to speed up recovery by adding a tablespoon of light kaolin to the dinner (or a smaller amount for a puppy). This is a harmless white powder, the basis of most proprietary products, which can be purchased without prescription. Store it in a sealed container. Arrowroot is another good home

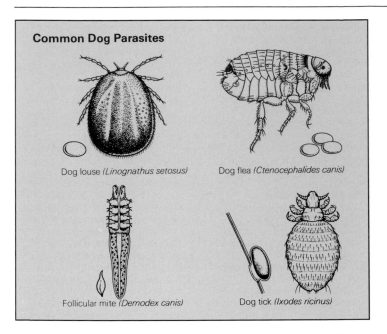

Common Dog Parasites

Dog louse *(Linognathus setosus)*

Dog flea *(Ctenocephalides canis)*

Follicular mite *(Demodex canis)*

Dog tick *(Ixodes ricinus)*

remedy also available from your chemist or pharmacy. To use, mix one tablespoon with a little cold milk and stir to a smooth paste; add more milk up to 1 pint (550ml) and stir well; boil as for egg custard and serve cool.

If the diarrhoea is not serious or prolonged, and the dog is not ill, it is probably better not to alter his diet but if it persists, it is better to change to a bland and easily digestible one. Rice pudding, egg custard, cooked macaroni, boiled egg, cottage cheese, plain yoghurt, boiled fish and chicken are all suitable. Do not restrict his intake of water or other fluids but do not let him drink too much at one time. This diet should be continued for two or three days before gradually returning to the normal feed.

If the diarrhoea is persistent or your dog looks ill, in that he is dull, listless, appears uninterested in everything around him or is off his food, it is possible that the diarrhoea is a symptom of something more serious, so seek the advice of your vet. Diarrhoea may also be due to stress — for example, the excitement of going to a dog show can cause it.

Above: *Four kinds of external parasites with their eggs. Though too small to see, these can cause your dog a lot of distress.*

Blood in the diarrhoea other than a slight fleck of blood on the outside of the stool, which may be due to straining, should serve as an alarm bell, particularly if you dog looks ill. It may well indicate a virus infection which will require immediate veterinary treatment, especially in the case of puppies, as it may indicate parvovirus or coronavirus.

SKIN PROBLEMS

Skin problems are unfortunately all too common with short-coated breeds such as the Dobermann. They can conveniently be divided into three categories — parasitic, fungal and allergic.

Parasitic
Parasites may be either internal or external. Internal parasites include roundworms and tapeworms and a number of less common worms. As these live in the intestine and steal

the dog's food he will appear to be in poor condition, with a dull, staring coat. The removal of the worms will generally remedy the problem, though it may take a few weeks for the dog to regain his normal condition. The regular control of worms has already been discussed, as have skin problems arising from the presence of external parasites and ringworm.

If you have eliminated parasitic or fungal causes, then you should suspect an allergy. The commonest allergy of Dobermanns is to beef or flaked maize. Try changing the diet, giving an egg on some soaked biscuit meal — this should be 100 per cent wheatmeal, as it contains a different vegetable protein. After a few weeks the symptoms should disappear. Veterinary advice should be sought if you are at all worried.

Inflammation of the skin is often referred to as eczema, which may be either wet or dry. Individual spots may sometimes appear for no apparent reason. These are best treated with tincture of iodine or by swabbing on demodoctic mange lotion. Spots under the chin are a common Dobermann problem and are a form of acne. These can often be cured very quickly by the application of methylated spirits on a cotton-wool swab.

MINOR INJURIES

Injuries are generally best left to your vet to treat, as he is not only able to assess speedily what action needs to be taken but has the necessary equipment and drugs with which to take it. However, many injuries are very minor and can be treated at home.

Cuts or bites which are bleeding should be washed very carefully with clean warm water with a little disinfectant and the bleeding can often be stopped with potassium permangagate crystals. Bandage the wound if necessary so as to apply pressure to the bleeding point. Do not tie a bandage too tight or it will act as a tourniquet and cut off the blood circulation.

Wounds to the ear flaps of uncropped dogs bleed freely and are difficult to stop, since the dog will keep shaking his head and starting the blood flow again. Stop the bleeding if you can, then surround the wound with cotton wool and bandage the ear to the side of the head.

Always keep a small bottle of antiseptic dusting powder from your vet for putting on small injuries. It will help to reduce the risk of infection and is better than antiseptic ointment, as it will keep the wound dry. If the damage has been caused by something that might introduce infection, such as rusty wire or a bite, it is a wise precaution to arrange for the dog to see the veterinary surgeon.

KENNEL COUGH

Kennel cough is caused by a combination of several viruses and bacteria and is most prevalent in the warmer summer months. Affected dogs develop a harsh rasping cough, but otherwise appear fit and healthy. It is more of a nuisance than a serious problem, other than with young puppies and the very elderly who may be at risk from developing pneumonia. The disease is normally transmitted by contact with an infected dog, but it may also be airborne in nature. If your dog develops kennel cough, you should keep him away from other dogs and consult your veterinary surgeon about a course of antibiotics.

Lick Sores
These are not uncommon on Dobermanns; they are sore places on the hocks (ankles) or carpal joints (wrists) caused by constant licking. They are frequently called boredom sores as they occur more on dogs which are left alone for long periods with nothing to occupy them. The best remedy is to remove the cause by changing the dog's life-style. If infected to any great degree the sores should receive immediate veterinary attention.

Chapter Five

TRAINING YOUR DOBERMANN

THE REASONS WHY

If you own a dog of any breed you should make the effort to train it. A well-trained dog is a happy dog, because it knows its relationship to its human family and can conform to the rules and procedures operated by that family. Training your dog is also a social necessity and is part of the responsibility that owning a dog puts upon you; your dog should always be under your control and should never be allowed to cause a nuisance to anyone else or to jeopardize public safety in any way. This is particularly important with a Dobermann, since it is a large energetic dog which often acts first and thinks afterwards. An untrained Dobermann could therefore cause you problems.

THE FIRST STEPS

Training Dobermanns is relatively easy, as they are highly intelligent dogs that learn very quickly.

From the moment you bring your puppy home, your relationship with him is in effect a continuous training session, though neither you nor he may realize it. The first things he will learn are to be clean in the house and to respond to his name and come when you call him. He will very quickly learn a whole number of other things, such as

when and where he is fed, where he is exercised, the boundaries of his territory, what behaviour is or is not acceptable and where he sleeps. With a little thought, this concept can be extended to enable you to train your dog at home to whatever level you consider necessary. In addition, obedience training classes are run in most areas. The basic objective of these classes is not only to train your dog but to teach you how to train him yourself at home. There are also likely to be specialist training classes for show-training, working trials and agility if you are interested in these activities.

The important thing to realize from the outset is that whatever you and your dog do together, you will be working as a team. Teamwork requires a strong bond of trust and loyalty between you which will gradually develop as the puppy grows older. The first requirement is that your hands give

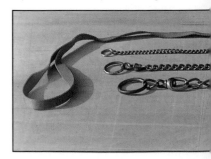

love and affection. Your puppy should always want to come to your open hands. You should therefore never hit your dog, even if he has played you up or been naughty — you should always be able to control your Dobermann with the tone of your voice. The Dobermann is a sensitive dog, so be careful how you correct him as it is very important not to break his spirit or damage the trust between you, particularly while he is still a young puppy.

OBEDIENCE TRAINING

Once your puppy has been inoculated you should arrange to take him to an obedience training class. Details of clubs running classes in your area can be obtained from your national kennel club, local dog breeders or even your local library. In addition to the many local clubs which cater for all breeds, a number of the Dobermann breed clubs also provide training classes. These may mean extra travel but the effort may be worth while, as you will be working with other Dobermann owners and their dogs and the trainers are likely to be more knowledgeable about the breed. Whatever club you attend, you will almost certainly need to become a member and pay a training fee for each lesson.

Most obedience classes aim to provide a general basic training for dogs and owners. If you enjoy obedience training and you are able to train your Dobermann to a reasonable level of proficiency, then you can have a go at entering obedience competitions. These may either be run within the training club or be open competitions for which you will need to enter in advance. Some training clubs cater particularly for those wanting to work their dogs competitively.

Obedience exercises taught in the training classes are generally based on those that you would be required to do in competitons. The exercises in the two lowest classes, Beginners and Novice, will include all the basic procedures that are needed to have a well-trained dog under proper control. These are walking at heel on the lead, sit, down, stay, come, leave and, at a later date, the retrieve. Higher classes will include working your dog off the lead, send-away, distance control and scent-work.

When working your dog in the training class you will be required to use a choke-chain. This is very effective as a training device, as it will enable you to have full control over your dog and will teach him to be responsive to your commands. While you will almost certainly be taught the correct use of a choke-chain, you should make sure that you only use one with large links. These will have the necessary corrective effect on the dog but are not likely to damage him. Fine-linked chains should always be avoided, as they can cause excessive pressure on the neck vertebrae which may, in extreme

Below: *A selection of chains. From the top — nylon lead; fine choke; two larger linked chokes and a semi-choke.*

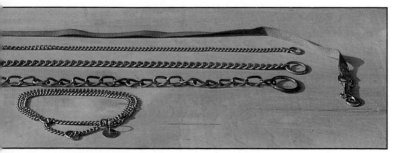

cases, lead to actual damage. Be extremely careful how you use a choke-chain when walking your Dobermann, as excessive use can again damage the neck vertebrae. You are also at risk of losing your Dobermann, as they can very easily slip their heads out of a choke-chain. A strong leather collar or a semi-choke is better and safer.

When attending obedience training classes, wear a comfortable outfit and avoid high-heeled shoes and loose flapping clothing. For your dog, you will need a large-linked choke-chain and a lead of about 4ft (12m) long, in addition to his normal secure collar.

Walking at heel

You can do the majority of the basic obedience exercises with your dog at home. Teaching him to walk at heel on a loose lead without pulling is essential if your walks are not to develop into a constant tug-of-war. This can be taught in the garden very quickly. Put him on a collar and lead (or use a choke-chain if you prefer) and simply walk him up and down. He should learn to walk on your left-hand side, on a loose lead, without pulling. Hold the lead in your right hand with just sufficient slack to take it lower down in your left hand. Each time he pulls away from you, give the choke-chain a sharp jerk with the left hand and release it as he comes back to heel, at the same time giving the command 'heel' or 'close'. Do not walk him on a tight lead, as you will lose the benefit of the choke-chain. Every few paces, change direction by turning 90° to the right, or 180° about-turn at the same time giving a firm command 'heel' or 'close'. As with all training,

Below: *Walking to heel is first taught on the lead, but can be done off the lead when the dog is more proficient.*

always give him praise when he does it correctly. He will very quickly learn to walk with you and watch for your instructions. Always keep talking to your dog as your voice will give him encouragement as well as commands. If you do not talk to him, he will not know what you want him to do.

Sit, down and stand

Once he is walking steadily at heel, introduce the command 'sit' into the heelwork. When you come to a halt, give him a firm command 'sit' and, if necessary, pull him back slightly on the choke-chain with the right hand and push his rear end into the sit position with your left hand. Once in the correct position, introduce the command 'stay', and keep him sitting for a few seconds. Again, praise him when he does it correctly.

As a variation, put him in the down position, with the command 'down'. If necessary, push his front end down with your right hand on the choke-chain and your left hand on the lower end of his back. With a little bit of encouragement, he will soon distinguish between sit and down. As a further variation, introduce the command 'stand'. If this is done from the sit or down position, simply walk him forward

Below: *Teaching the 'sit' is part of basic heelwork and is most important to ensure control in any circumstance.*

one pace until he is in the stand position. His enthusiasm to cooperate with you and to do it right will be increased greatly if you have a pocket full of titbits such as chocolate drops which you can use as rewards.

Stay

The next exercise to master is the stay. He should already have a basic understanding of this from his heelwork. Keeping him on the lead, put him in the sit position and, having given a firm command 'stay', walk to the end of the lead then turn to face him. Keep giving the 'stay' command and, if he obeys, return to his side after about 30 seconds, continuing to give the command if necessary. On completion of the exercise, give praise and a reward.

Recall

Once mastered, the stay exercise can be extended to include the recall. Leave him in the sit position as before, but once you are facing him at a lead's length away, give him the command 'come' and encourage him to come to the front of you and then to sit. If necessary, pull on the lead as you say 'Come'. The recall distance can be increased by taking a few paces back as he is coming towards you. It is conventional in the recall exercise for the dog to 'finish' by going round behind you in a clockwise direction and ending in the sit at heel position on your left-hand side. This would be taught at any

Left: *The first stage in teaching the command of 'stay' — the dog is safely on its lead and facing the handler.*

Below: *The first stage in teaching the 'recall' off the lead. Note the hand command in addition to voice control.*

training class and would be required in competition, but for normal home training is not strictly essential. Once he has grasped the recall, this can be done off the lead.

The hall or landing is an ideal place to teach this, as it is an enclosed space giving less opportunity for him to decide that the whole thing is boring and rapidly disappear. Heelwork off the lead is also best taught in the hall, since it gives a sense of enclosure and thus less temptation for him to stray too far from you. Once the basic control exists, you can try it in the garden.

The retrieve
The traditional retrieve article used

Below: *The 'recall' is another essential command to teach, since your dog must always come to you when called.*

in most training classes is the dumb-bell. You can teach this at home very easily by making it a game.

Use any handy article such as a stick, a small log or even an apple. The retrieve exercise requires the dog to pick up the item you have thrown and bring it back to you. The first is easy to achieve, since any dog's instinct is to do just this. The more difficult part is in persuading him to retrieve. Use a combination of recall command and a

---

Below: *The 'retrieve' is an essential part of competition obedience, but a Dobe will soon tire of its repetition.*

happy, excited tone of voice, which emphasizes that it is a game rather than a serious exercise. Once he has returned the item to you, always praise him. Like any of the training exercises described, never do it for too long, since a Dobermann tends to have a low boredom threshold and soon loses interest. The best recipe to avoid this is little and often.

Scentwork
Many obedience training clubs are very stereotyped in what they teach within any particular class, which is a great pity. Never be afraid to teach your Dobermann the more advanced exercises when he is still young or before he is particularly

Above: *The dog is required to pick up the dumb-bell after it has been thrown and bring it back to the handler.*

Below: *Having retrieved the dumb-bell, the dog must hold it while sitting in front of the handler until it is taken away.*

Above: *Retrieving can be taught early on as a game using a variety of articles such as apples and dog toys.*

proficient at the more basic exercises. Scentwork is rarely taught at training classes until the advanced classes. It is, however, one of the easier exercises to teach at home. Start with your bag of rewards. Make him sit beside you and stay, holding his collar if necessary, throw a reward across the room, then tell him to find it. The speed with which it disappears will soon tell you that he knows the rules of the game. Next, cover his eyes with one hand so that he does not see you throw the reward, then tell him to 'find'. He will be only too anxious to do this and will soon be using his nose to track it down. Once this stage has been mastered, leave him in one room, hide the reward in another room and then send him to find it. The hiding places can get progressively harder so that he really has to hunt for his prize. This is actually teaching him to use his nose to pick up the smell of the reward and his eyes to find a hidden article.

The next stage is to move on to matchboxes. Put a reward in an empty matchbox, place it at one end of the room, then send him to retrieve it.

Once he has returned it to you he will have earned the reward. You will need to use your powers of voice control to give him suitable encouragement to bring the matchbox to you rather than destroy it. Once achieved, place about six new boxes of matches from a sealed pack on the floor, spaced about 6-12 inches (15-30cm) apart. These will carry no scent. Place the by now heavily scented box with the reward in it amongst them, then tell him to 'find'. If he picks up any of the decoy boxes, tell him 'no', but he is likely to go straight for the right one. Once retrieved, he will again have earned the prize and your thankful praise.

This routine can be great fun and is surprisingly easy to teach. He will have learnt to select one item with a known scent on it from amongst a number of scent-free items (which is the basis of all scentwork exercises) and to use his nose to find hidden articles, which is something he will need to know if you ever do working trials.

Send-away and distant control

The two other advanced exercises, the send-away and distant control, can also be taught at home if you wish, though these are more difficult and of little benefit unless you intend to enter serious obedience competition. The send-

away involves making the dog go away from you for a distance of about 10ft (3m), then waiting, either in the sit or down position, until you call him back to you. This is difficult to teach, since going away from you is contrary to all his instincts. In competitions, the dog

Below: *Send away and distance control are more advanced, to be taught only when basic obedience has been mastered.*

Bottom: *In the 'send away' exercise, the dog goes away from the handler on command to a pre-arranged spot.*

is required to go away from you into a clearly marked-out area. Distant control involves making the dog sit, down or stand at a distance. He should be able to alternate from any one position to another and to move to the left or to the right on command while at a distance from you. Initially, all commands will be given with the voice but these can be replaced with hand signals once your dog is well trained. It is always a good idea to use hand signals in conjunction with voice commands from the outset, in order to make the transition easier.

OBEDIENCE COMPETITIONS

If you find that your Dobermann does good obedience and you enjoy working with him, then have a go at competing in an obedience competition.

It is best to start with competitions organized within your training club or even match-competitions between local clubs. If you do reasonably well and you both enjoy it, then try an open obedience competition. For this, you will need to obtain a schedule from the organizing club and enter prior to the stated closing date. Competition is likely to be against a wide variety of breeds and to be very keen. Each exercise carries a set maximum number of marks and the judge will deduct marks each time your dog makes a mistake, such as not sitting straight or getting up while he is supposed to be sitting. The dog which loses the least marks will be the winner.

Never allow such competitions to assume too much importance. If your dog makes a mistake or lets you down, do not take it out on him. He is only doing his best or at least, what he thinks he ought to do. ·

If you want to own a Dobermann and to do obedience with it, fine. If your primary interest is in doing obedience, then take my advice and don't buy a Dobermann. Alternatively, buy a breed more suitable for obedience work in addition to your Dobermann. Doing precision obedience on a regular basis, particularly when it is raining or cold, or there are other interesting things happening nearby, is not a Dobermann's idea of fun.

WORKING TRIALS

If you are interested in utilizing your Dobermann's intelligence to the full you should consider doing Working Trials. These are, in essence, an extension of the exercises that you will already have done at your obedience training classes (without your dog having achieved a reasonable degree of proficiency at obedience it would be very difficult to start doing working trials).

In Britain there are a number of Working Trials training clubs which run classes. In addition, several of the Dobermann Clubs also run training classes and this may be your best starting point. Most people who train their dogs do so in order to take part in competitions or to qualify their dogs at the various Working Trial Stakes. The training you receive will therefore be directly related to the exercises that you would do in Working Trials competitions.

There are three categories of Working Trials. These are Championship Working Trials (which are open trials at which Kennel Club Working Trial Certificates are offered), Open Working Trials (which are open to all, subject to the limitation on the maximum number of dogs permitted to take part) and Members Working Trials, which are restricted to dogs owned by members of the club promoting the trial competition.

The Working Trial competitions are called Stakes and the five Working Trial Stakes, in ascending order of difficulty, are Companion Dog (CD), Utility Dog (UD), Working Dog (WD), Tracking Dog (TD) and Police Dog (PD). A dog must achieve a certain level of success in one Stake before moving on to a higher one.

Chapter Six

SHOWING AND THE STANDARDS

SHOWING YOUR DOBERMANN

Dog showing is a very enjoyable hobby for many people and its popularity has increased considerably over recent years. Today, there are more shows than ever before and they command a much larger entry.

If you decide to show your Dobermann you must look at it as a sport and the most important objective must be to enjoy yourself. There is no magic about a show dog — most Dobermanns which are shown are basically family pets. In practice, in fact it is probably true to say that many of the best dogs, in terms of their show potential, are never shown.

To some people, winning is so important that it becomes almost a matter of life or death. This is very sad, because dog showing should be done for the pleasure it gives you. It is a competitive sport.

Competition

When you show your Dobermann you will be in competition with a number of other dogs, possibly of many different breeds. You will be attempting to convince the judge that your dog is better than all the other dogs in the ring. To do this, you will need to present your dog to its best possible advantage.

The judge will assess each dog against the breed standard for its particular breed and at the same time compare it against every other dog in the ring. The winner will be the one that the judge considers most nearly matches its breed standard. In practice, every judge will interpret the breed standard differently; his interpretation may be influenced by his own dogs, a dog he particularly admires or by the way the dog is handled and presented.

PREPARING FOR THE SHOW RING

If you decide to show your Dobermann, enter an Exemption Show or a local Open Show and simply have a go. In the USA, Fun or Sanction matches give beginners a chance to try their new puppies under actual show conditions. Experienced breeders will also use these as a training ground for their own puppies. It does not matter if you make errors, or even if you mess it up totally. Everyone makes mistakes when they start, even the most experienced exhibitors occasionally!

Treat your early shows as a training ground for both yourself and your Dobermann. Learn from your experiences and from what other exhibitors are doing. Never be afraid to ask for help — most people will be only too glad to advise you. Dobermann exhibitors are, by and large, friendly and helpful, but if you do not request their aid you cannot expect them to take the initiative.

Even if you don't show your dog very well you may still win something, as judges make allowance for bad handling, giving greater weight to the quality of the dog. However, where two dogs are of equal merit, handling is likely to make the difference.

You can enter Exemption or Match Shows on the day but for other shows you will need to obtain a schedule and send in the entry form by the stipulated closing date. Make sure you enclose the appropriate entry fees. Championship Shows generally send out entry passes prior to the day, but others rarely do so unless they are being run in conjunction with other events such as agricultural shows. Your dog will need to be registered with your national Kennel Club and transferred to your name in the Kennel Club records. If you need any help regarding registration or transfer of ownership, ask the Kennel Club. If you need guidance about how to enter dog shows, ask the experienced exhibitors at your ringcraft or handling class.

On the day

Having entered a show, it is your responsibility to be in the ring when required. It is a good idea to arrive at the show some while before your class is due in order to let your dog settle down and absorb the show atmosphere. Most dogs are tense and excited at first. It is particularly important to arrive early if you are showing a puppy, as not only do they need longer to settle themselves, but the puppy classes are generally the first to be judged.

Make sure that you wear something comfortable which will not flap around and disturb your dog. This particularly applies to ladies, who should also wear flat-soled shoes. It can be very difficult to show a Dobermann and keep control over it effectively when you are wearing a loose skirt and high-heeled shoes.

Although conformation is always likely to take precedence over presentation, dog showing is a beauty competition. You should

Below: Presenting Roanoke Flair, an experienced show dog. Note the minimal physical contact and fine chain accentuating the shoulder.

therefore ensure that you are smartly dressed and that your dog is properly prepared. Make sure that you clean his teeth, clip his nails if they are too long, brush his coat and remove any scurf which may appear, particularly around the neck — this usually manifests itself just as you are about to go into the ring and is due to the dog's tension. There are a number of products which you can use to remove scurf and to put a finishing shine on the coat. Remember, it is an insult to the judge to take your dog under him without the proper preparation. Do not bath him prior to every show unless it is absolutely essential as this will remove the natural oils from the hair and may leave him with a dry, harsh coat.

Many exhibitors believe it is necessary to remove the dog's whiskers in order to give a cleaner line to the head. This is a fallacy — a judge rarely notices whether or not the dog is wearing his whiskers as he has only a limited time in which to assess the dog's conformation.

It is conventional to show Dobermanns on a long, fine-linked choke-chain. This is not used as such, but is merely employed to emphasize the lay-back of shoulder, thereby giving the impression of a good reach of neck and a short length of back. The choice of lead is very much one of personal preference. The majority of exhibitors use nylon leads because they are soft in the hand, light and very strong.

Make sure that you keep good control over your dog. Always anticipate what he is likely to do and be ready to react. Equally, you will need to be ready for what other dogs may do. The majority of Dobermanns are very amenable and there is generally little belligerence in the ring, though one lively dog can often stir up others. Greater care needs to be taken with the males than the females.

Equipment
You will need a show-bag in which to carry your show equipment. You will soon learn from experience what you need, but the list is likely to include the following items:

Below: *An alert, attentive expression is very much desired when the time comes for your dog to be judged in the show ring.*

show chain and lead; benching chain; soft hand glove or chamois leather; coat spray; benching rug; first aid kit, mainly for the dog; ring bait; towel; refreshments for yourself and your dog, including water and a drinking bowl.

Some of the outdoor shows can be very cold and you should always take clothing to meet any climatic conditions. Don't forget a coat for your dog — it is not cissy to put a coat on a Dobermann. It is a short-coated breed which can feel the cold, particularly if it is also raining. Remember, you dog is your greatest asset — without him you wouldn't even be at the show, and you want to keep him fit and healthy in order to show him again.

The Championship Shows and many of the larger Open Shows in the UK are benched, in that each dog has his own compartment where you can put him during the show. You will need a blanket of some description for him to lie on and a benching chain with which to secure him. You will also need a strong collar. You should never bench your dog on a choke-chain in case he falls off the bench and strangles himself. You should also ensure that he is benched on a fairly short chain.

You must always display your ring number in the ring. This will either be given to you as you enter the show or be handed to you by the steward as you enter the show ring with your dog.

Catalogues are available at shows, other than Exemption Shows. These set out details of each dog and list which are entered in each class. The catalogues are useful on the day in order to enable you to follow what is going on and they are also a good source of reference for the future (particularly those from Championship and Club Shows) as they contain details about the breeding of each dog.

TRAINING FOR THE SHOW RING

Showing a dog is one of those things that looks deceptively easy when you watch it being done by an expert. In reality, showing in the ring is the end-product of much training and hard work. It can be very frustrating, as many dogs behave beautifully at home or at the training class, but fail to keep to the rules as well as you would wish when in the ring. This is an instance where practice makes perfect — keep training and showing your dog and keep trying to learn and you will both improve.

Ringcraft classes
If you intend to show your Dobermann you would be well advised to attend ringcraft or handling classes. Like obedience classes, these are held in most areas. Details can be obtained from the Kennel Club or your local canine society.

Many of the ringcraft classes are run by canine societies as a service to their members. Membership is relatively cheap and may also benefit you in obtaining reduced price entry fees for the societies' shows. It is usually mandatory, as most societies have insurance policies to cover them for any legal liability arising from any actions by the dogs owned by their members. In addition to membership, you will have to pay a nominal sum of money each week to cover the costs of running the classes.

The standard of a training class depends very largely on the quality of the trainer. Ideally, the trainer will be able to teach you all you need to know about how to show your dog. Ringcraft classes are also ideal for socializing your dog. This is an important aspect, because your Dobermann will have to acustom himself to being in a show ring with numerous other dogs and taking no notice of them. He will also have to accept being handled by people he does not know. The earlier you commence this socializing the better. Take your puppy to ringcraft classes as soon as he is inoculated at, say, 14 to 16 weeks old. It does not matter if he only sits and watches to begin with. Don't push him too fast — let him find his feet in his own time.

Apart from training your dog to show, you should study the breed standard and learn what it means. It is even more important that you study your own dog and learn his good and bad points. This is something that you will probably only learn through experience by watching at the ringside and by talking to other exhibitors. Only when you know his faults and virtues will you be able to learn how to extol the latter and hide the former, which is where the real skill and experience come into play. It is important that your dog is not shown so as to reveal faults that he does not have, through your inability to handle properly or through ignorance. Some faults cannot be hidden; others can be minimized by clever handling.

Training your puppy

Training should start at about seven weeks of age. Stand your puppy on a table-top and get him used to being placed in position and having to stand still. At this age, puppies readily accept this discipline. Do not over-do it; just a few minutes training at a time, then lots of praise and a reward. It must not seem like a punishment. Once he has learned to accept a collar and lead, get him used to being 'stood up' on the floor. If necessary, place his legs so that he is standing four square. You should use the commands 'stand, stay'. Most exhibitors have some form of ring bait in order to hold the dog's attention — the most popular one is cooked liver, cut into small pieces. Use a piece of cheese, a biscuit or anything he likes and encourage him to stand for the bait. This will make him pull himself up and reach forward while remaining standing. This is the stance he will need to take when in the show ring, and the earlier he learns it the easier it will become. If you do use bait in the ring, be discreet with it. Do not scatter it around the ring, as this will distract other dogs, and do not feed your dog just as the judge is about to look in his mouth.

Your training class will give you the opportunity of practising this standing routine in something approaching a show atmosphere, with the excitement of other dogs and people around, and all the ringside noise. It will also enable you to teach your dog to trot up and down on a loose lead without becoming distracted. You should both learn to become totally flexible, in that you can do anything that you might be required to in the show ring. Once you start showing, after your dog reaches six months of age, showing and training can go hand in hand. The training classes will help you to overcome any presentation problems, such as the dog not moving in a straight line, backing off from being handled, and so on.

THE ART OF SHOWING

Many exhibitors are very nervous when they show their dogs. This is a natural state of mind, but it is one that you must learn to control. Apart from making you hot and flustered and preventing you from showing your dog to his best advantage, your tension is likely to go down the lead to the dog, making him apprehensive too. You will then both be feeding off each other's tension. You will hopefully become less nervous with experience and it may help you to remember that no-one is looking at you — they are too busy looking at your dog.

Learning the 'stand'

The first lesson to master is how to stand your dog. The objective is to stand him four-square so as to enable the judge to assess his conformation. The convention is to stand him facing to the right when you are standing behind him. Hold the lead in your right hand, keeping it fairly short so that it does not trail on the ground, otherwise you will get tied up with it. Use the right hand to hold the dog under the chin by placing your fingers gently in the groove between the lower jaw bones. This will leave the left hand free for placing the dog's legs in the required position and for giving him the necessary self-confidence by handling him. Keep talking to him both to give him the commands 'stand and stay' and to praise and reassure him.

Using the left hand, place the front leg nearest to you so that it is at right angles to the ground. Then lift slightly under the chin with the right hand, which will enable you to move his front left leg and to place it parallel to the right one. Next place the right hind leg — the one nearest to you — so that the hock is at right angles to the ground. Move your left hand under the dog, and place the left hind leg parallel to the right one. The left hand is thus still free to adjust the dog's position if necessary and to stroke him to give him confidence. Do not over-stretch the back legs, as this will make him look long in the body and over-angulated in the

hindquarters. It will also result in the front legs being too far forward, making him appear shallow-chested, as the elbows will no longer be held close to the chest.

Make sure that the front legs are parallel and that the feet turn neither in nor out. Check that the back legs are also parallel; do not let him stand cow-hocked, especially if he does not actually have this fault. It is a good idea when you have placed your dog, to come round to the front to see that he is standing in a straight line. If he is standing off-line he is likely to move, possibly at the critical moment when the judge is looking at him. It is also worthwhile to walk round the other side to check what the judge will see.

Having learnt to stand your dog four-square, you can either 'top and tail' him, free-stand him or use a combination of the two methods. With a puppy, it is probably better to adopt the top and tail method; this is also ideal for inexperienced dogs or for those which do not free-stand properly. The top and tail method does enable you to show the true conformation of your dog and to create the image that you want the judge to see, i.e. a level topline, high tailset, well-laid shoulders and a good reach of neck. It is also a good method to use where the dog shows no interest in bait and indicates that he would prefer not to be in the ring by looking bored by the whole procedure. Such a dog should not be shown free-standing, since his lack of attention will be clear for all to see and will reduce your chances of success.

The top and tail method is generally done by standing the dog

Above left: *A German Dobe standing four-square on a loose lead. Its cropped ears are the norm in America and Europe.*

Left: *Ch. Star Dobes Irish Fantasy, an American champion illustrating the US method of show presentation.*

as already described, then switching the lead to the left hand and baiting the dog forward with the right hand. The left hand can raise the tail if required and readjust the legs and feet if necessary. This involves very little handling of the dog and enables you to see clearly the profile you are presenting to the judge, while at the same time baiting the dog in order to create the impression of alertness and cooperation. Once he has learnt to hold this stance, you can reduce the physical contact to a minimum until you are virtually free-standing him. On no account should you drop the lead in the ring, whichever way you are showing your dog.

The logical step from this is to move to the front of your dog so as to face him and bait him from that position. You should check carefully that your dog is standing correctly on a loose but controlled length of lead, and that you are presenting the outline that you want the judge to see. All too often, exhibitors get a wonderful, keen expression but fail to realize that the whole stance of the dog is wrong. Ensure that the head is not too high or held back too far, as this will make the dog look as though he has a short neck, a straight shoulder and, quite possibly, a dipping topline as well. Do not simply free-stand your dog because it is considered to be the best way to do it — make sure that it really does enable you to do justice to your dog. It is a good idea to co-opt a friend to help you by checking that your dog is standing correctly when you are in the process of showing him.

Learn to stack your dog facing the 'wrong' direction, i.e. head to your left when he is standing in front of you. This is essential, since you must always ensure that as the judge is moving around, the dog is between the two of you. There may be instances when this requires the dog to stand facing the opposite direction.

You should also learn to read the ground at outdoor shows. Never stand your dog facing down a slope

— always face him up it. Use your common sense, however; facing your dog in the reverse direction could cause problems if it results in two dogs standing nose to nose, particularly if they are two males in a crowded ring. Nevertheless, you may be able to utilize any slope in the ground when presenting your dog to the judge. You will have to teach your dog to accept this reverse stance, as it is very easy for a dog to learn how to stand in the ring but to be completely lost when asked to do something different. Your dog must learn to be flexible and adapt to anything that may be required of him.

Judging
When your turn comes for your dog to be judged you should stand him four-square so that the judge can run his hands over him, checking his temperament, dentition, conformation and physical condition. If your dog is inexperienced or backs off from the judge during this laying on of hands, you are unlikely to win, as the judge will probably consider that your dog has a questionable temperament.

If this ring shyness persists, you will need to make great efforts to overcome it. Keep taking him to training classes and encourage everyone to go over him — this need be no more than simply coming up to him and running a hand over him. In addition, you will need to work more closely with him. As the judge approaches, keep your right hand under his chin and your left hand on his head, so maintaining maximum physical contact. Give him firm commands to 'stand, stay', as well as plenty of vocal encouragement and praise. Most dogs that back off will do so as the judge approaches, so aim to keep him steady during this period.

Once the judge starts to handle the front of your dog, keep on talking to him and keep handling him from a position just behind the shoulder so as not to interfere with the judge. As the judge moves alongside your dog, you should

Above: *Crufts 1988, Dobermann Ch. Sallate Ferris being judged in the Working Group after having already won Best of Breed.*

move back to a position alongside his head, continuing to use hands and voice. You can relax your close handling as the judge moves away.

Backing off is not uncommon in young dogs and may be due to poor temperament, the handler being nervous, inexperience, or over-enthusiastic handling by the judge. Young dogs often go through a temporary silly stage at about 9-12 months; this is part of their growing up and the problem normally resolves itself fairly quickly. Sometimes, however, the true temperament only manifests itself at about this age. If backing off is due to faulty temperament you may never overcome it, but you should aim to control it. Standing the dog in the reverse position (head to the left) during judging, sometimes stops him backing off.

Movement

Having examined your dog, the judge will ask you to move him. This should be done at the trot, so you will need to practise before you go into the ring to make sure that he can do it under control. You may only get one chance, so do not waste it; move him at a steady speed on your left side on a loose lead.

Movement is a very important part of the judging process. It is not done simply to see if the dog

moves nicely, but in order to help the judge assess the conformation. Obviously, the better a dog moves, the better his conformation is likely to be. Many faults show up when a dog is moving which can be hidden by careful handling when he is standing.

The judge will normally watch the dog moving from the front and the rear by asking you to take the dog away and back to him in a straight line. He will also want to see the dog's movement in profile, so will either ask you to trot your dog in a triangle so that he can see him from the front, rear and side, or to take him in a circle around the ring. It is conventional to move your dog on your left side, though you should always ensure that the dog is between you and the judge. This may necessitate moving with the dog on your right side, so you should train your dog to be happy on either side of you. Always move in a straight line, otherwise the judge will not be able to assess whether your dog is sound in front and rear.

Use a loose lead, so as not to impede the free-flowing movement of your dog. Use plenty of encouragement to hold the dog's attention, mixed with sufficient commands to make him gait freely alongside you. Anticipate when you approach the corners of the ring. Use your voice and if necessary your left hand to guide your dog around corners. You must learn to do this without him breaking his rhythm. If possible, don't let your dog trot up and down as if it were a chore — try to add a bit of style and panache. A little flamboyance never comes amiss; presentation and style will always count in your favour.

It is better not to have any bait in your hand when moving, as this may encourage your dog to watch your hand, thereby moving at a slight angle to the direction of travel; this is often known as 'crabbing'. As your dog becomes more experienced, this is less likely to be a problem. Judges will often ask you to let your dog stand free at the end of the movement and here it is useful to let the dog think you have bait in your hand, even if you have not. It will make him stand free in an interested fashion, using his ears and wearing that pleasingly alert facial expression which so many judges seem to want. You should also check that he is standing relatively correctly, so if necessary walk him into a better stance.

Pacing is a bad habit which dogs occasionally adopt in the ring, so always watch your dog's movement to make sure he is not doing this. Pacing is a waddling movement in which the dog moves his legs in parallel sequence rather than alternating the front left/rear right legs with the front right/rear left legs as he should in the trot.

Pacing is normally easy to overcome and two methods are worth trying. Step off with a firm command and a slight jerk on the lead. This will make him lead off on one foot, thereby breaking straight into the trot. Alternatively, turn round in a tight circle with your dog and move off as you complete the circle. Pacing in the ring will prevent the judge from assessing

the dog's movement and thus his conformation. It may therefore cost you any chance of winning.

When moving, your dog should be encouraged to keep his head up rather than following a scent on the ground. Do not string your dog up on a short length of chain at the top of his neck as this will tend to throw his front movement out of balance. You will need to learn the correct speed at which to move your dog. Aim for the speed at which he moves freely and rhythmically.

Do not over-work a young dog in the ring. It must be an enjoyable experience for him. If you keep stacking him up all through the class he may lose interest and not show to advantage towards the end, when the judge is making up his mind as to his winners. The same applies to an older dog to some extent, but you must remember that the judge may look round the ring at any moment and see your dog standing free, thereby catching something that you would prefer him not to see and may have tried carefully to hide — e.g. a narrow front, soft topline or low tailset. Also remember that many future judges will be at the ringside, all of whom will be watching your dog. (It is equally true that the judge is also being judged by the ringside — a fact that too many judges forget too often!)

Awarding the prizes

Once the judge has finished assessing the class and made up his mind he will place his winners, in his order of preference. These dogs will each receive a prize card or ribbon and, at some shows, a rosette. Prize money may also be given, but this is becoming less common every year. It is important to remember that you have not won anything until the judge has entered his placings in his judging book and you have received your prize. Many an award has been lost by an exhibitor relaxing too soon, allowing his dog to stand at ease and reveal faults.

Judges are often accused of

Above: *Rosettes provide a permanent memento of show ring successes; here are just some won by the Roanoke Dobermanns.*

judges like a medium-sized elegant dog, whereas others prefer a much larger or, indeed, much heavier, stockier dog. Each judge is right, in that it is his interpretation of the breed standard.

The only way to ascertain whether your dog is up to show standard is to show him and see what happens. Do not take the opinion of just one or two judges; take a consensus opinion of a number of them. A good dog will tend to be placed at most shows, whereas a poor dog will not. As you will very soon realize, judging is very much a subjective affair. If you lose out on the day, don't be critical of the judge; you may disagree with him, but you cannot say he is wrong. Accept your successes with joy and your defeats with good grace.

THE BREED STANDARD

Ask anyone what a Dobermann looks like and they would probably say that it is a tall dog of elegant outline, with a short smooth coat, black and tan in colour and a docked tail. Whilst this would probably be sufficient to give a general idea of what a Dobermann looks like, it would provide no information on how tall it should be, what shape the head should be, how long or short the body should be, or indeed what any particular part of the dog should look like.

What a Standard is

The Breed Standard sets out to describe just that. It describes what a Dobermann should look like when it competes in the show ring and may thus be described as the official description of the breed. In practice, this actually describes what the ideal conformation of the Dobermann should be to enable it to do the work for which it was created.

The importance of the breed Standard cannot be over-emphasised, since it is the basic blueprint to which breeders, exhibitors and judges work. Without it, everyone would aim to

being biased towards winning dogs, people they know or dogs from certain sires or bloodlines. Such accusations even extend to favouring certain handlers because they are well-known or have a reputation for always winning. Generally speaking, such accusations are merely the ringside murmurings of unsuccessful exhibitors. Judging is nearly always fair in that you get what you ask for — the judge's opinion of your dog. This opinion may vary from show to show and from judge to judge. A judge may give an award to a dog he has previously not placed; this could be due to the dog being more mature, being in better condition, showing better or simply being up against easier competition. Therefore, if a judge does not place your dog you should not decide not to show under that judge again.

Experience will teach you what type of dog any individual judge will go for and they certainly do have preferences. Some Dobermann produce their own ideal Dobermann and the breed as we know it today would cease to exist.

Breed Standards are drawn up initially by the Breed Clubs and are then approved, with or without modifications, by the Kennel Club. The Breed Clubs can ask their national Kennel Club to amend the Breed Standard whenever they feel it to be necessary. Where there is a Breed Council, as there is with Dobermanns, such a request can only be made after the membership of the member clubs of the Breed Council have considered the

suggested amendment and the majority of them are in favour of the amendment. The Kennel Club in Britain will normally agree to such requests, but they themselves retain the right to alter Breed Standards. The Kennel Club also tends to modify the more extreme wishes of the clubs, e.g. by not allowing any fault to be a disqualifying fault.

How it is organised

The British Breed Standard is divided up into 18 sections and a concluding note covering the

Below: *A stylized diagram of the Dobermann, showing some of the most important bones of the skeleton.*

1 Skull 2 Cervical vertebrae 3 Thoracic vertebrae 4 Lumbar vertebrae 5 Sacral vertebrae 6 Coccygeal vertebrae 7 Pelvis (hip bone) 8 Hip joint 9 Femur 10 Patella 11 Fibula 12 Tibia 13 Hock 14 Tarsals 15 Metatarsals 16 Phalanges 17 Phalanges 18 Metacarpals 19 Carpals 20 Ulna 21 Radius 22 Sternum 23 Humerus 24 Ribs 25 Scapula

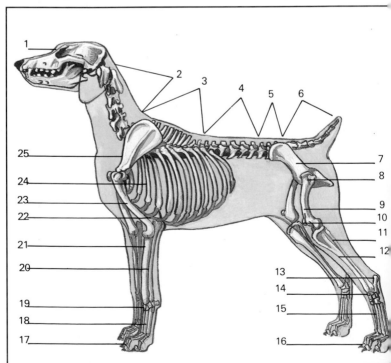

various component parts of the body. These give a brief description of what each part of the body should look like and how they should integrate together to form the complete Dobermann. In some instances it is quite specific as to what is required but in others it is very general. This means that it is open to varying interpretations which are often matters of opinion rather than fact. A situation which enables individual judges to express their own personal likes and dislikes, yet still remain within the limits of the Standard.

THE SKELETON

The skeleton is the framework upon which the rest of the dog hangs. Since any faults in the skeleton will result in corresponding faults in the conformation of the dog, it is of fundamental importance to the Breed Standard. Whilst it is not necessary to have a detailed knowledge of the skeleton in order

to understand the Breed Standard, it is helpful to have some idea of the basic components and the relationship between its various parts. Similarly, it is helpful in understanding the Standard, to have a general idea of the anatomy of the Dobermann.

The UK Standard
General appearance Medium size, muscular and elegant, with well set body. Of proud carriage, compact and tough. Capable of great speed.

Characteristics Intelligent and firm of character, loyal and obedient.

Temperament Bold and alert. Shyness or viciousness very highly undesirable.

Head and skull In proportion to body. Long, well filled out under eyes and clean cut, with good depth of muzzle. Seen from above and side, resembles an elongated blunt wedge. Upper part of head flat and free from wrinkle. Top of skull flat slight stop; muzzle line extending parallel to top line of skull. Cheeks flat, lips tight. Nose solid black in black dogs, solid dark brown in brown dogs, solid dark

Below: *The UK Kennel Club made tail-docking optional in 1986, but the majority of Dobes still have docked tails.*

grey in blue dogs and light brown in fawn dogs. Head out of balance in proportion to body, dish faced, snipy or cheeky very highly undesirable.

Eyes Almond-shaped, not round, moderately deep set, not prominent, with lively, alert expression. Iris of uniform colour, ranging from medium to darkest brown in black dogs, the darker shade being more desirable. In browns, blues, or fawns, colour of iris blends with that of markings, but not of lighter hue than markings; light eyes in black dogs highly undesirable.

Ears Small, neat, set high on head. Normally dropped, but may be erect.

Mouth Well developed, solid and strong with a complete dentition and a perfect, regular and complete scissor bite, i.e. the upper teeth closely overlapping the lower teeth and set square to the jaws. Evenly placed teeth. Undershot, overshot or badly arranged teeth highly undesirable.

Neck Fairly long and lean, carried with considerable nobility; slightly convex and in proportion to shape of dog. Region of nape very muscular. Dewlap and loose skin undesirable.

Forequarters Shoulder blade and upper arm meet at an angle of 90 degrees. Shoulder blade and upper arm approximately equal in length. Short upper arm relative to shoulder blade highly undesirable. Legs seen from front and side, perfectly straight and parallel to each other from elbow to pastern; muscled and sinewy, with round bone in proportion to body structure. Standing or gaiting, elbow lies close to brisket.

Body Square, height measured vertically from ground to highest point at withers equal to length from forechest to rear projection of upper thigh. Forechest well developed. Back short and firm, with strong, straight topline sloping slightly from withers to croup; bitches may be slightly longer to loin. Ribs deep and well sprung, reaching to elbow. Belly fairly well tucked-up. Long, weak, or roach backs highly undesirable.

Hindquarters Legs parallel to each other and moderately wide apart. Pelvis falling away from spinal column at an angle of about 30 degrees. Croup well filled out. Hindquarters well developed and muscular; long, well bent stifle; hocks turning neither in nor out. When standing, hock to heel perpendicular to the ground.

Feet Well arched, compact, and cat-like, turning neither in nor out. All dewclaws removed. Long, flat deviating feet and/or weak pasterns highly undesirable.

Below: *The angles of conformation for the forequarters. The length of the shoulder (A) should be equal to the upper arm (B).*

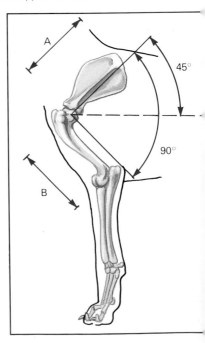

Tail Customarily docked at first or second joint; appears to be a continuation of spine without material drop.

Gait Elastic, free, balanced and vigorous, with good reach in forequarters and driving power in hindquarters. When trotting, should have strong rear drive, with apparent rotary motion of hindquarters. Rear and front legs thrown neither in nor out. Back remains strong and firm.

Coat Smooth, short, hard, thick and close lying. Imperceptible undercoat on neck permissible. Hair forming a ridge on back of neck and/or along spine highly undesirable.

Colour Definite black, brown, blue or fawn (Isabella) only, with rust red markings.
   Markings to be sharply defined, appearing above each eye, on muzzle, throat and forechest, on all legs and feet and below tail. White markings of any kind highly undesirable.

Size Ideal height at withers: Dogs 69 cms (27 ins); Bitches 65 cms (25½ ins). Considerable deviation from this ideal undesirable.

Faults Any departure from the foregoing points should be considered a fault and the seriousness with which the fault should be regarded should be in exact proportion to its degree.

Note Male animals should have two apparently normal testicles fully descended into the scrotum.

The US Standard

General conformation and appearance
The appearance is that of a dog of medium size, with a body that is square; the height, measured vertically from the ground to the highest point of the withers, equalling the length

Below: *The correct angles of conformation for the hindquarters. The hocks should be at 90° to the ground*

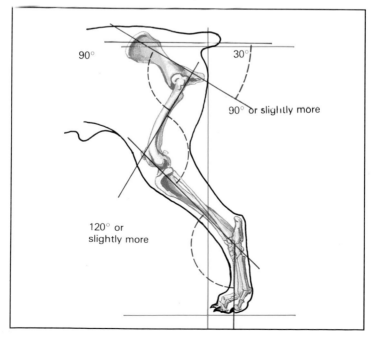

90°

30°

90° or slightly more

120° or slightly more

Above: *US and British Dobes are basically the same. The most obvious difference is the cropped ears of the American.*

measured horizontally from the forechest to the rear projection of the upper thigh.

Height At the withers. **Dogs** 26 to 28 inches, ideal about 27½ inches. **Bitches** 24 to 26 inches, ideal about 25½ inches. Length of head, neck and legs in proportion to length and depth of body. Compactly built, muscular and powerful, for great endurance and speed. Elegant in appearance, of proud carriage, reflecting great nobility and temperament. Energetic, watchful, determined, alert, fearless, loyal and obedient.

The judge shall dismiss from the ring any shy or vicious Doberman.

Shyness A dog shall be judged fundamentally shy if, refusing to stand for examination, it shrinks away from the judge; if it fears an approach from the rear; if it shies at sudden and unusual noises to a marked degree.

Viciousness A dog that attacks or attempts to attack either the judge or its handler, is definitely vicious. An aggressive or belligerent attitude towards other dogs shall not be deemed viciousness.

Head Long and dry, resembling a blunt wedge in both frontal and profile views. When seen from the front, the head widens gradually toward the base of the ears in a practically unbroken line. Top of skull flat, turning with slight stop to bridge of muzzle, with muzzle line extending parallel to top line of skull. Cheeks flat and muscular. Lips lying close to jaws. Jaws full and powerful, well filled under the eyes.

Eyes Almond shaped, moderately deep set, with vigorous, energetic expression. Iris, of uniform colour, ranging from medium to darkest brown in black dogs; in reds, blues, and fawns the colour of the iris blends with that of the markings, the darkest shade being preferable in every case.

Teeth Strongly developed and white. Lower incisors upright and touching inside of upper incisors — a true scissors bite. *42 correctly placed teeth,* 22 in the lower, 20 in the upper jaw. Distemper teeth shall not be penalized.

Disqualifying Faults Overshot more than 3/16 of an inch. Undershot more than ⅛ of an inch. Four or more missing teeth.

Ears Normally cropped and carried erect. The upper attachment of the ear, when held erect, is on a level with the top of the skull.

Neck Proudly carried, well muscled and dry. Well arched, with nape of neck widening gradually toward body. Length of neck proportioned to body and head.

Body Back short, firm, of sufficient width, and muscular at the loins, extending in a straight line from withers to the *slightly* rounded croup. **Withers** Pronounced and forming the highest point of the body. **Brisket** Reaching deep to the elbow. **Chest** Broad with forechest well defined. **Ribs** Well sprung from the spine, but flattened in lower end to permit elbow clearance. **Belly** Well tucked up, extending in a curved line from the brisket. **Loins** Wide and muscled. **Hips** Broad and in proportion to body, breadth of hips being approximately equal to breadth of body at rib cage and shoulders.

Tail Docked at approximately second joint, appears to be a continuation of the spine, and is carried only slightly above the horizontal when the dog is alert.

Forequarters; Shoulder Blade Sloping forward and downward at a 45-degree angle to the ground meets the upper arm at an angle of 90 degrees. Length of shoulder blade and upper arm are equal. Height from elbow to withers approximately equals height from ground to elbow. **Legs** Seen from front and side, perfectly straight and parallel to each other from elbow to pastern; muscled and sinewy, with heavy bone. In normal pose and when gaiting, the elbows lie close to the brisket. **Pasterns** Firm and almost perpendicular to the ground. **Feet** Well arched, compact, and catlike, turning neither in nor out. Dewclaws may be removed.

Hindquarters The angulation of the hindquarters balances that of the forequarters. **Hip Bone** Falls away from spinal column at an angle of about 30 degrees, producing a slightly rounded, well filled-out croup. **Upper Shanks** At right angles to the hip bones, are long, wide, and well muscled on both sides of thigh, with clearly defined stifles. Upper and lower shanks are of equal length. While the dog is at rest, hock to heel is perpendicular to the ground. Viewed from the rear, the legs are straight, parallel to each other, and wide enough apart to fit in with a properly built body. **Cat Feet** As on front legs, turning neither in nor out. Dewclaws, if any, are generally removed.

Gait Free, balanced, and vigorous, with good reach in the forequarters and good driving power in the hindquarters. When trotting, there is strong rear-action drive. Each rear leg moves in line with the foreleg on the same side. Rear and front legs are thrown neither in nor out. Back remains strong and firm. When moving at a fast trot, a properly built dog will single-track.

Coat, color, markings: Coat Smooth-haired, short, hard, thick and close lying. Invisible gray undercoat on neck permissible.

Allowed colors Black, red, blue, and fawn (Isabella). **Markings** Rust, sharply defined, appearing above each eye and on muzzle, throat and forechest, on all legs and feet, and below tail. **Nose** Solid black on black dogs, dark brown on red ones, dark gray on blue ones, dark tan on fawns. White patch on chest, not exceeding ½ square inch, permissible.

Disqualifying fault Dogs not of an allowed color.

Faults The foregoing description is that of the ideal Doberman Pinscher. Any deviation from the above described dog must be penalized to the extent of the deviation.

Disqualifications Overshot more than ¾ of an inch. Four or more missing teeth. Dogs not of an allowed color.

Section Two

BREEDING A DOBERMANN

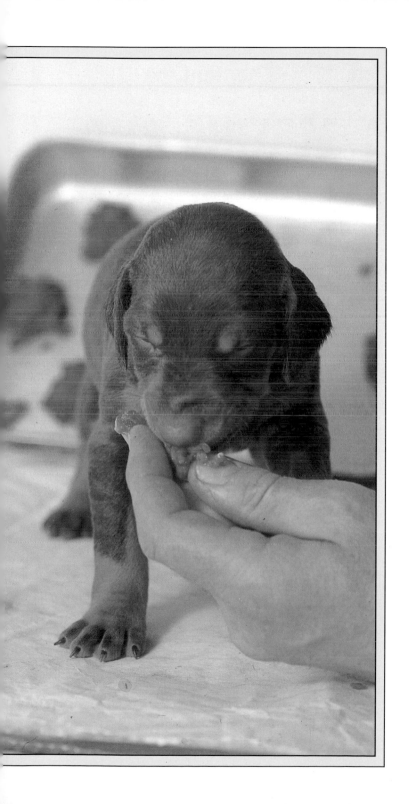

Chapter One

MATING AND WHELPING

BREEDING OR NOT

Before you make the decision to breed, check whether there is likely to be a realistic market for your puppies. The rapid rise in popularity of the Dobermann over recent years has resulted in a corresponding increase in the numbers of litters being bred. If other people in your area are having difficulty in selling puppies, you may be wiser to decide not to breed any yourself. There is nothing more heartbreaking than breeding a lovely litter of puppies and finding that no one wants them. It is also worth considering at what time of the year your puppies would be ready to sell; if this is likely to be near Christmas or during the summer holidays, it may be prudent to defer the litter until a more propitious occasion.

If you do decide to breed from your bitch you should aim to produce as good quality a litter as possible. This means puppies with sound conformation and steady temperaments which people will be proud to own. If your own bitch has poor conformation or temperament, she is likely to produce poor puppies, so you should refrain from breeding from her. Those who breed poor quality litters from poor quality stock are not really breeders — they are merely producers.

Having decided to become a breeder, you should ensure that you never exploit your bitch. Never mate a bitch until she is about two years of age. Never breed litters from two consecutive seasons unless the previous litter was very small — three puppies or fewer. Never breed from a bitch once she reaches seven years of age — and never breed from a bitch of any age which is not in good breeding condition.

THE CHOICE OF STUD DOG

Having decided to mate your bitch, you will have to decide which stud dog to use. This is a very important decision, as it will determine what your puppies will look like. It should therefore only be made after a lot of thought.

Line-breeding is often advocated as the best way to breed. This involves mating the bitch to a dog within the same family, possibly the grandfather, a half-brother or a dog of similar breeding to the bitch. The theory is that by mating close relatives you double-up on their genetic material, so establishing a dominant line. It also increases the chances of producing a litter of puppies which will all be of similar type, both to each other and to the parents. Line-breeding can only be done if a suitable line-bred stud dog exists, and should only be considered where the available dog is sufficiently sound. Such a mating would obviously be no good if both the dog and the bitch have the same fault, since it would also be inherited by the puppies. If the dog has an undesirable trait it should also be avoided, since you do not want to introduce faults into your breeding.

Very close line-breeding, such as mating brother with sister, is known as inbreeding. This should be avoided unless you are a very experienced breeder with a detailed knowledge of the dogs' pedigrees and can be quite sure that there are no undesirable traits that would be magnified.

The alternative to line-breeding is out-breeding, where there is little or no common breeding in the two pedigrees. Out-breeding gives you the opportunity of assessing all the available stud dogs and selecting the one which you think will give you the best quality litter. This is frequently done in the hope that you will achieve puppies that are of a higher standard than the bitch. A stud dog of similar type to the bitch can be used if you want the puppies to be like the mother.

Selecting a stud
Do not use 'the dog round the corner' even though the stud fee may be cheap and it is close to home unless you are really sure that it is the right dog to use. When considering any potential stud dog

you should study its pedigree and, if necessary, seek advice as to the quality of its ancestors. Many reasonable-looking dogs are the culmination of several generations of indiscriminate breeding, so are likely to produce a wide variety of types in their litters. Beware also of using the fashionable dog or the current winning dog, unless you are sure that he is descended from sound stock and is himself producing good quality offspring. The best results are often obtained from a well-bred, sound dog, whether or not it is a successful show-dog. If your choice of stud dog is dependent on other factors, such as his ability to produce a particular recessive colour, then your choice is correspondingly reduced. It is unwise to breed purely for colour at the expense of quality — you should aim to breed for both.

If you are not familiar with the various dogs and their bloodlines you should visit some of the larger dog shows and study the various dogs exhibited. Alternatively, there are a number of reputable kennels which will house sound stud dogs, often descended from generations of selected breeding. These can

Below: *To help avoid potential whelping problems later, your bitch should be in first-class shape before mating.*

usually be visited by arrangement with the owner.

Once you have made the all-important decision, you should approach the stud dog owner well in advance and seek his agreement to the intended mating. He may wish to see your bitch or have details of her pedigree, so be prepared to make a preliminary visit. If he is amenable, you should tell him when the bitch is due to come into season, which you should know from your own records. You should also agree the stud fee in advance, as well as any other terms which you might make.

Negotiating the fee

The normal procedure is for a stud fee to be paid to the owner of the stud dog upon completion of the mating. Be careful about agreeing terms, such as giving a puppy or pick-of-the-litter in lieu of stud fee — such terms often cause problems (such as when only one puppy is born) and are likely to be more costly to you in the long run, since the average stud fee is about half the price of a puppy.

Your stud fee is the payment for the use of the stud dog and is not dependent in any way on the results of the mating. You will not be entitled to any refund if the bitch does not produce a litter, although it is normal practice however, to allow a free return mating at the next season. This is not a right, however, so you should check at the outset that this option will be available to you if need be.

Having made your decision, you will have to back your judgement and in time the resultant litter will show whether or not that judgement has been correct.

THE BITCH

Bitches normally come into season at six-monthly intervals, each season lasting about 21 days. It is not known what brings bitches into season, but light and temperature are believed to be important factors. There are occasions when considerable numbers of bitches of different breeds appear to come into season earlier or later than expected. There are some bitches that only come into season once every year, and others that come into season every four months. Such bitches need careful watching if a breeding programme is being planned.

The breeding cycle

The first stage of the cycle is that the bitch begins to secrete the hormone oestrogen. As the oestrogen level increases, it causes the bitch to come into season in the next few days. As this happens, the vulva enlarges and it is at this point that the bitch becomes attractive to dogs. This attraction is enhanced by the bitch urinating far more frequently. In the early part of the season, the urine contains a scent which presents a clear signal to males. As a bitch comes into season she generally becomes more excitable, so care needs to be taken if you have several bitches together, apart from the obvious need to separate the bitch from any males for the duration of the season.

Apart from causing the enlargement of the uterus, the rise in the oestrogen level causes an increase in the blood supply to the uterus and vagina. The small blood vessels within the vagina then rupture, which leads to the characteristic blood-stained discharge which indicates that the bitch is in season. The first day that this discharge is present is generally taken to be the first day of the season. It is important to watch carefully for this, as some bitches are particularly clean and can conceal it for several days. A bitch may occasionally have a dry, or clear, season in which there is little or no evident discharge. This does not indicate any problem and such bitches will produce litters in the normal way, provided they are mated on the correct day.

By about the tenth day, the oestrogen level begins to fall and another hormone, progesterone, begins to increase. This causes the vulva to soften and open, so making the bitch physically receptive to the dog. At the same time, actual ovulation begins. The objective is to mate the bitch at the time of maximum ovulation, or slightly before.

THE MATING

It is up to the owner of the bitch to select the right day for the mating; the stud dog owner's responsibility is to ensure that the bitch is mated. Selecting the 'right' day, i.e. the day when the bitch is ovulating and so is ready for mating, can be very difficult. With Dobermanns this is usually between the tenth and thirteenth days, but they can be ready for mating as early as the second day and as late as the twentieth. Only if the bitch does not conceive after matings on the conventional days is it worth trying earlier or later in the next season. Many claimed cases of infertility in bitches are due simply to the bitch being mated on the wrong days. In such cases, varying the time of mating should be attempted in preference to hormone treatment, though this is always available as a last resort.

Judging the moment

There are three main pointers which are helpful in deciding when the bitch is ready for mating. The main indicator is the reaction of the bitch when you run your hand along the back towards the tail. If she is receptive, the tail will be pushed to one side. The vulva will become softer and more open, and the discharge will change from a bright blood-red colour to a paler, straw colour. None of these indicators are infallible, however, so should never be relied upon totally. Some bitches turn their tails all through their seasons, while others retain a bright red discharge until the season ends. This does not indicate a problem and has no effect on the fertility of the bitch.

It is normal procedure to take the bitch to the stud dog, as he is more likely to mate successfully on his own territory (although an experienced stud dog will probably have sufficient self-confidence to perform in almost any environment — I have even witnessed a mating between the occupants of adjoining benches at a dog show!

It is best to mate the bitch twice, leaving 48 hours between the two matings. This will enable a wider range of the bitch's season to be covered, so increasing the chances of catching the day of her maximum ovulation.

Payment of a stud fee does not give you an automatic right to expect two matings, so you will need to clarify that this is acceptable to the stud dog owner at the outset.

If the bitch appears to be receptive earlier than the tenth day, then mate earlier; the later part of the season will still be covered. It is always possible that her early readiness merely indicates that you missed the true beginning of the season.

Visiting the stud

Exercise your bitch immediately prior to the mating to ensure that she is comfortable, but preferably not in the stud dog's territory. He has to live with the smell long after the bitch has gone home.

The mating should be carefully stage-managed so as to achieve a successful tie quickly and with as little upset to the bitch as possible. To the uninitiated, this may seem like organised rape, but it is, in reality, the kindest and most efficient way of achieving the desired result. The concept of the dog and the bitch running free in the garden and mating after a natural courtship is a very attractive one but is totally unrealistic.

The owner of the stud dog will expect the bitch to be muzzled before the mating. A dog lead or a crepe bandage looped over the muzzle and round the back of the neck makes a simple but effective muzzle. This is generally only required until a tie has been achieved, and is to ensure that the bitch does not take fright

The mating is actually done in some convenient but secluded place such as the garage, depending upon circumstances. It is better for the stud dog if all his mating is done in the same place. The owner of the bitch normally sits on a chair and holds the front of the bitch steady, while the stud dog owner holds the back-end of the bitch and offers such assistance to the stud dog as he may need. A well-trained stud dog should need little or no help.

The dog will mount the bitch and once he has penetrated her will effect a tie, which will last any time from 12 minutes to 30 minutes, though 20 minutes is about normal. Both dog and bitch should be held steady during this time to ensure that the bitch does not attempt to pull free through excitement or apprehension. The sperm is passed into the bitch a few minutes after the dog has penetrated her. This means that it is possible for conception to occur without a tie though this can by no means be guaranteed. If there is no tie, the mating should be considered unsuccessful and no stud fee paid. After the sperm has been ejaculated, the dog passes a fluid which is produced by the prostate gland and which washes the sperm through the cervix into the uterus. If the dog produces a lot of this prostate fluid, some may escape from the bitch's vagina once the tie is broken. This is of no consequence and no attempt should be made to stop it.

Once the mating has been completed the bitch is likely to be in a state of great excitement, so should be kept quiet until she settles down again. Keep her well clear of other males, as a second mating to a different dog would result in a mixed litter, some being sired by each dog. Such a litter is difficult to register and can cause many problems later, not least the inability to provide a pedigree.

Gestation

The gestation period for any breed of dog is 63 days, which means that the puppies should be born on or about 63 days after the day of the mating. Most Dobermann litters tend to be born between the sixty-first and sixty-third days, though I have experienced a bitch whelping a perfectly normal litter of puppies 10 days early. You would be well advised, therefore, to be ready and waiting at least one week before the duly appointed day. Litters that are overdue are of much greater concern. Although they can be born several days late, it is certainly a cause for anxiety if nothing has happened after the sixty-fifth day.

EARLY PREGNANCY

You are unlikely to be able to tell whether your bitch is actually in whelp until about three weeks after the mating. In fact with some Dobermann bitches carrying small litters, it really can be almost impossible to tell the difference between a litter and a false pregnancy. At about this time, however, there are four indicators to watch for which may give you a clue. The teats will have begun to enlarge and will be more prominent than normal; the vulva will have remained soft and open, rather than contracting as normal; the appetite may be larger than normal; and the bitch may also begin to show subtle behavioural changes around the house, such as climbing carefully on to the couch instead of leaping on to it. She is unlikely to show any physical evidence of swelling at this stage of the pregnancy.

Some vets are able to tell on examining a bitch at about the twenty-first day after the mating whether or not she is in whelp.

On balance, I do not consider that it is worth asking your vet to examine your bitch at any stage during the pregnancy unless you think that she is ill. She is best left well alone. If she is in whelp, you will find out soon enough and in plenty of time to make all the necessary preparations.

Even if you do not take your bitch to see the vet, it is a good idea to tell him that she is due to whelp on a particular day and to seek his confirmation that he is willing to give you assistance should it be needed. Vets seldom object to helping on these occasions but they may object to being called out in the middle of the night to a whelping that they know nothing about. It is a matter of common courtesy, as well as being good public relations. You should also bear in mind that while he may be willing to advise you, he is unlikely to stay and help you whelp your bitch. That is something that you will have to do yourself. Also, many vets have had little experience of breeding and whelping; their expertise is in treating sick animals.

Booster vaccinations

There are differing opinions as to whether booster vaccinations, particularly for parvovirus, should be given to the bitch once it has been mated. A booster gives the bitch a high level of immunity, resulting in the puppies also receiving a high antibody level from the bitch. While this may appear to be a desirable objective, it may well be counter-productive. Puppies are usually vaccinated at 12 weeks,

because by that age the maternal antibody level has normally worn off, so making them totally receptive to the vaccination. Where the maternal antibody level is too high, however, it will still be present in some degree at 12 weeks, resulting in the vaccination not taking. This risk is particularly high in the Dobermann, which tends to retain a sufficiently high parvovirus antibody level, often up to six months of age, to prevent the vaccination from giving the required protection. The only way to be really sure would be to blood test the puppies two weeks after each vaccination to measure the antibody level, and to keep giving boosters until the required antibody level is reached.

It is therefore better not to give the bitch a booster within three months of being mated or during the pregnancy. The puppies will then derive a moderate level of antibody protection and be receptive to the normal 12 week

Below: *Embryos gestating within the horns of the uterus. They will stay here for 63 days, until separating at birth.*

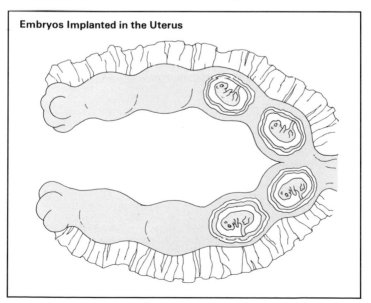

Embryos Implanted in the Uterus

vaccination. However, if you feel
that there is a genuine risk of the
puppies being exposed to
parvovirus at an early age, it is
obviously a good idea to increase
their antibody level. You must, in
that case, warn the eventual
purchasers of the puppies in order
to avoid them vaccinating the
puppies at 12 weeks and believing
them to be adequately protected.

Worming
A bitch that is wormed regularly at
six-monthly intervals is unlikely to
have any active roundworms in the
gut. However, it is a good idea to
worm your bitch before she is
mated to ensure that she is free of
worms.

Even though the bitch may have
no worms, she will pass worm
larvae through the placentas to the
puppies.

Exercise
During the first three weeks of the
pregnancy the bitch should
continue very much as normal so
far as both feeding and exercise are
concerned. She should be allowed
to take what exercise she wants,
without being forced to do more.
Some exercise is essential in order
to keep the bitch in good condition.
A fat, sluggish bitch with poor
muscle tone is much more likely to
have whelping problems than one
which is in good hard condition.
Care must be taken, however, not
to over-exercise as a thin bitch has
less body reserves to draw upon
when rearing the litter. Do not
expect to get your bitch into good
condition after she has been mated.
This is much too late — you should
get her into good condition well in
advance. Better still, she should
always be in perfect condition. If
the bitch is not in peak condition,
she should not be mated.

LATE PREGNANCY

By about the sixth week, you
should start to see your bitch
thickening in the flanks. By this
stage, she should be beginning to
look matronly and should be

slowing down. Even so, you may
not be really sure whether she is in
whelp, though you should be
getting a good idea. From the sixth
to eighth weeks, the bitch will really
show physical evidence of a litter.
Not only will she continue to fill out
in the flanks, but her underline will
begin to drop. By now, you should
know whether or not you have a
litter on the way.

Between the third and sixth
weeks you should continue to give
adequate exercise, but it is now
more important that this should be
carefully regulated. This means that
you will have to start thinking for
her and not allow her to go racing
round and round for long periods of
time. You should also take every
precaution to ensure that she does
not bang herself and so risk
damaging or even losing her
puppies. From the sixth week, the
bitch should be allowed minimal
exercise only. She will take what
exercise she needs, which will
probably be limited to walking
round the garden.

Feeding
Feeding should be very much as
normal until about the fifth week.
At this stage, the amount of food
given should be increased from the
normal 2-2½ lb (0.9-1.1kg) per day
to about 3-3½ lb (1.3-1.5kg),
prepared weight. If you are feeding
a meat and biscuit diet, the protein
content should be increased and
the carbohydrate content reduced
as a percentage of the total diet to
give an approximate 50/50 ratio.
The protein intake can best be
increased by giving additional meat,
eggs, milk and cheese. Avoid too
much raw milk as this will cause
diarrhoea; it is best given cooked,
in the form of egg custard.

Do not give too much bulk as
this is likely to fill the stomach,
resulting in pressure being exerted
on the enlarging uterus and so
causing discomfort. If the bitch is
very enlarged towards the end of
the pregnancy, it is better to divide
the total food to be given into two
or even three smaller meals. As a
consequence of this, the bitch will

need to relieve herself more frequently, so you will have to be prepared to let her out into the garden at regular intervals. She will certainly need to urinate more frequently in any case, as a result of her kidneys functioning for both herself and the unborn puppies, and because of the pressure on the bladder from the uterus.

If you are feeding a well-balanced diet there is not likely to be any need to give additional minerals or vitamins.

Most people give too many additives which the bitch cannot utilise and which are therefore wasted. A small amount of additional calcium can be given from the sixth week onwards. This is best given in the powdered form, with a total of about half a tablespoonful per day being sprinkled on to the food. This will help the bitch in the development of the puppies, though it will not prevent eclampsia (see page 102).

This is due to a change in the blood calcium level, usually caused by the sudden withdrawal of milk by the newborn puppies.

The final stages
It is not unusual for the bitch to have a slight discharge from the vagina during the last three weeks of the pregnancy. This is generally a clear or white mucus and should not cause any concern. If the discharge is blackish in colour it does signify that there may be a problem and you should seek veterinary advice as soon as possible. This should not be confused with the greenish-black fluid which will be present during the whelping.

During the final week you should be ready for action at a moment's notice. It is a period of waiting.

WHELPING EQUIPMENT

There are a number of things that you will need to get ready prior to the actual whelping. You should certainly be prepared at least one week in advance of the date the litter is due.

The first decision to make is that of accommodation. Where is the bitch going to whelp and rear her puppies? Whether you are going to whelp inside the house or in an outside building, the principles are the same. The bitch will prefer a small room, shed or kennel which gives her a sense of enclosure and is private, in that it is not going to have people in and out all day and will be quiet. This will become her sanctuary and she will be more at ease if she knows that she will not be disturbed, particularly by other dogs and people outside the immediate family. The room should be capable of being kept at a temperature of about 70°F (21°C). It is essential that this temperature is maintained from about one week prior to whelping until the puppies are five or six weeks of age. Hypothermia is one of the main causes of fading puppies, and the main reason why so many puppies die young.

Below: *A standard wooden whelping box with pig rail, overhead infra-red lamp and low stool as a working seat.*

The whelping box

The major item of equipment that will be required is the whelping box. This is where the puppies will be born and reared, and may serve as a convenient bed for them once they have been weaned. Ideally it should be made of wood, as it is strong, can withstand a considerable amount of chewing, is not cold to the body and can be thoroughly cleaned after use, ready for the next litter. Cleanliness is important and for this reason it is most unwise to borrow a whelping box, since this may introduce cross-infection.

The whelping box must be large enough to accommodate a bitch and a litter of fast-growing puppies. It needs to measure about 3ft 6in x 3ft 6in (1m x 1m) with sides of about 10in (25cm) in height. The front should be left open in order to allow easy access, but should be fitted with a rebate, enabling loose boards to be slid into position. This will enable the front boards to be put in place if necessary, such as when you want to box the puppies inside. Alternatively, you can put in a low board which will keep the bedding in the box without forming an unnecessary obstacle for the bitch. A pig-rail should be fitted to the inside of the box. This is simply a wooden bar fixed to the back and the two sides of the box, designed to enable any puppies that get behind the bitch to crawl back to safety, without getting squashed by her. The rail should therefore be fixed about 6in (15cm) above the floor of the box, so that the bitch will lie against it. The whelping box should be raised at least 1in (2.5cm) off the floor in order to allow ventilation under the box and to deter vermin.

Heating

Heating the whelping room is best done by means of an electric infra-red heater connected to a thermostat. This should be placed sufficiently high to be out of reach of the bitch. If it is to be used in a wooden building it will need to be fixed to the wall with a backing sheet of a non-flammable material such as asbestos. There are many other forms of heating which may be used, but it may be more difficult to regulate the temperature. Heating appliances such as paraffin heaters should not be kept burning for a long period in an enclosed environment — not only do they present a fire hazard if knocked over, but they give off dangerous fumes. A thermometer should be placed in the room in order to check the temperature.

In addition to the main room heater, you will need an overhead infra-red lamp. These are made specifically for the rearing of puppies and are relatively inexpensive; it would be worthwhile to acquire one at the outset, as it will last you for many years. Buy one designed to take up to a 400 watt bulb, as this is ideal for use in cold weather. In warmer weather, a 300 watt bulb will be adequate. Make sure that the bulbs are 'dull emitters', in which the heating elements are set in clay. Glass bulbs should not be used as these are liable to shatter, scattering hot glass into the whelping box. The lamp should be securely suspended from a hook in the ceiling on a length of chain, so as to give a pleasant radiant glow over the puppies. With a piece of wire bent to make an s-hook, the lamp can be raised or lowered by the required amount simply by placing the s-hook into a higher or lower link of the chain.

The incubator

You should make an incubator, which will provide a safe refuge for the puppies during the whelping. It will also be useful if you need to divide the litter into two. In its simplest form, this can be a cardboard box with a blanket inside it and a blanket or towel over the top. If it is cold, a hot water bottle can be placed under the bottom blanket. A thermostatically controlled plate warmer under the blanket is even better, since a regular degree of warmth can be maintained.

Other items

You will need to make some provision for yourself, as you will have to stay with the bitch for the last few nights of her pregnancy in order to be ready to render assistance when she starts to whelp. You will also need to stay with her for the first few nights after she has whelped. If you are able to watch adequately from your own bed, so much the better. Otherwise, a folding camp-bed and some blankets or a comfortable chair of some description should suffice. Also, a short-legged stool alongside the whelping-box is an extremely convenient seat from which to work.

Apart from the whelping box, the bitch should have access to her own bed. She will not want to leave her puppies for the first 10-14 days but after that will appreciate being able to get away from them. This need will increase as the puppies become older and more mobile. If her bed is in the whelping room it should be raised about 6in (15cm) off the ground to prevent the puppies from climbing into it.

A nightlight is always useful. All that is needed is a 5-8 watt nursery bulb in an inspection lamp, or some other light-fitting, which can be plugged into an electric socket. This should be left on every night until the puppies are about 6 weeks of age. Initially, it will enable the bitch to see the whereabouts of the puppies and later it will help the puppies to find their way back to bed at night. This should be supplementary to the normal room lighting, not a substitute for it. You will certainly need good lighting in the room during the whelping.

Other items of equipment which you will need to have in the whelping room include the following:

A pair of scissors Preferably with blunt ends to ensure that no unintentional damage is done with the sharp points.

A pair of artery forceps Also known as Spencer-Wells forceps, or clamp forceps. These have a number of uses apart from whelpings, such as cleaning ears.

Newspaper This will need to be clean, and as you will need quite large quantities, collecting should start well in advance.

Paper sacks Old dog-meal sacks are ideal, as they will not be contaminated in any way. About six will probably be sufficient.

Below: *Essential items of whelping equipment. The bitch's bed provides a convenient working surface.*

Kitchen roll A roll of absorbent paper has many uses.

Blankets Two or three old blankets, which should be washed and well dried before use.

Washing facilities If washing facilities are not available close to the whelping room a washing-up bowl, soap, hot water, cold water and a towel should be provided. You will need to wash your hands during the course of the whelping.

Paper and Pencil In case you need to make any notes about the whelping.

PRE-WHELPING

Having assembled everything that you think will be required, you will need to keep a careful watch on your bitch. As the whelping day approaches she will become less active and, if she is carrying a large litter, may become very uncomfortable. Make sure that she is kept well away from other dogs that may want to play rough, as you do not want to risk any damage to the unborn puppies.

Most bitches whelp in the small hours of the morning, but as with everything else in nature there are no set rules — she could start whelping at any time. There are some useful signs to watch for which may give an indication of when the action is likely to begin.

The day before whelping she will probably ignore all food and become very restless. She may frequently pass small amounts of faeces; this 'bopping' is quite characteristic. She will also be looking for somewhere to make a bed ready to receive the puppies; this is the time to take her to the whelping box, as you do not want her to start whelping on the living room couch, or even in the garden.

Bitch and the box

It is a good idea to get her used to being in the whelping box before she actually starts to whelp. This is particularly so if she is to whelp in an unfamiliar place. Putting the infra-red lamp on over the box is often an inducement, as she will be able to bask under the warmth. There is no need to force her to stay in the whelping box, as she will certainly not want to leave it once the puppies are in it. Open out two paper sacks and place them on the floor of the whelping box, cover it with several sheets of newspaper and a blanket on the top. Once she starts to whelp, the blanket should be removed, as she may well scratch the newspaper into shreds. Do not worry about this — it is quite normal procedure, though not all bitches do it. As you will find out, there is no such thing as a definite pattern of behaviour — every bitch is different in some way or another. It is normal, however, for the bitch's temperature to drop to about two degrees below normal just prior to whelping.

When the bitch is showing these symptoms of an imminent whelping, lay out the artery forceps and scissors on a work surface nearby. These should be both clean and sterilised — this can be done by boiling them in a saucepan of water for a few minutes. While awaiting use, they can be stood in a jar of methylated spirits to cover the blades, in order to ensure that they remain sterile until needed. Have a pile of paper towels and opened-out newspapers ready. Place an empty paper sack in the corner of the room in order to collect up all the dirty paper and rubbish during the whelping. This can then be disposed of afterwards.

THE WHELPING

The pre-whelping restlessness and bed-making may continue for several hours, though with some bitches it may be virtually non-existent. The whelping itself begins with the onset of abdominal contractions. Immediately prior to birth, each puppy is inside a water-filled bag joined to the placenta by the umbilical cord, with the placenta itself attached to the wall of the uterus. Until the contractions cause the bag (the amniotic sac) to separate from the uterus wall, the puppy is still technically a foetus.

Once it has become detached, further contractions push it out of the uterus, through the cervix (which by now will have opened to allow the puppies out) and expel it from the bitch, at which moment it is said to be born.

The contractions may begin several hours before the first puppy is born, though with some bitches the period may be only a few minutes. They may be relatively mild and somewhat intermittent initially and be interspersed with bouts of scratching up the bed. Do not assume that there is something wrong because the contractions continue for several hours without any results. This is where your patience is needed and rewarded.

The bitch may produce the puppy while she is lying down in the whelping box, or she may push it out from the standing position. The latter course does pose the risk of the puppy being damaged by being dropped on to the floor of the whelping box so you should be ready to catch it, with a piece of paper towel in your hand in order to prevent it from slipping out away from you. You may need to restrain the bitch so as to keep her steady while you receive the puppy.

Presentation

The normal presentation is head first and feet downwards. It is quite common for puppies to arrive tail first, with hind legs extended back, and this does not appear to cause any problems. These are sometimes wrongly referred to as breech births — a breech birth is in fact where a puppy presents tail first with the hind legs tucked under the body. Again, these do not usually cause problems, though the puppy may take longer to arrive. Occasionally one may be born on its back with its feet upwards.

Sometimes a puppy will get stuck half out of the vulva. This may be due to abnormal presentation or because it is larger than average. With a paper towel in your hand, help the puppy out by gently but firmly stroking it downwards. This downward pressure should coincide with the bitch's contractions. Do not pull the puppy out if it is not ready to come out on its own, as this may well cause it some damage. If the puppy is presenting upside-down, i.e. feet upwards, gentle pressure should be applied in the same way, except that it will be upward pressure. This will support the weight of the puppy and prevent any spinal damage as it is being expelled.

The puppy is normally born inside the amniotic sac, so will appear as a black cylindrical sausage. If so, break the sac with your fingers and wipe out any fluid or mucus from the nostrils and mouth with a small swab of cotton wool. Sometimes the sac will break before the puppy is born; in this case the amniotic fluid will be released and will gush out ahead of the puppy. This is not normally a problem, so long as the puppy is born relatively soon afterwards.

After the birth

The puppy may be expelled still attached to the placenta by the umbilical cord, or it may become detached first. If it is still attached, the artery forceps should be clamped on to the cord about 1in (2.5cm) from the puppy, and the cord cut on the side of the forceps furthest away from the puppy. The forceps only need to be left on the cord for a few seconds, as the cramping action will very quickly stop the flow of blood. Once they are removed the puppy should be placed alongside the bitch and she should be encouraged to lick it dry. You should assist in this operation by rubbing the puppy vigorously, but gently, with paper towels. This rubbing and the bitch's licking should stimulate breathing and the expansion of the lungs. This is often accompanied by the puppy squealing, which is therefore always a good sign. Once the puppy is reasonably dry, try to get it to suck from one of the bitch's teats. Some suck vigorously from the start, whereas others need lots of encouragement. If necessary, very gently open its mouth and

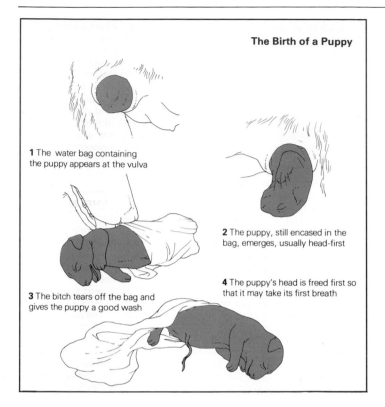

The Birth of a Puppy

1 The water bag containing the puppy appears at the vulva

2 The puppy, still encased in the bag, emerges, usually head-first

3 The bitch tears off the bag and gives the puppy a good wash

4 The puppy's head is freed first so that it may take its first breath

place it on to the teat in order to encourage feeding.

It is now time to clear up, ready for the next arrival. Any dirty paper and placenta should be placed in the rubbish sack. You may find that a considerable amount of fluid and blood is produced with the puppy. The bitch will want to clean this up, but it is better to cover it with additional sheets of newspaper. If left on her own, the bitch would eat the placenta. This is a valuable source of food to the bitch and is rich in minerals. However, it is better not to allow her to eat all the placentas as they will most certainly make her motions very loose and unpleasant. She will inevitably eat some, but this will do her no harm.

The second delivery
The interval between puppies varies from bitch to bitch. The normal range is 20-60 minutes but again there is no such thing as a definite

Above: *Encased in a membrane, the puppy is expelled from the vulva. Once born, the bitch licks it clean to start it breathing.*

rule. The bitch should be encouraged to rest until the next arrival; you will get advance warning of this by the commencement of further contractions. If the bitch resumes scratching up her bed, remove the first puppy to the sanctuary of the incubator. If she settles down again it can be returned to her, but you should be ready to remove it again when necessary. Eventually the second puppy will arrive, and you should go through the same procedure as before. The first puppy may well be the most difficult one to produce as it will need to stretch the passageway, thus making it easier for the subsequent puppies to follow.

Upon completion of the second delivery, return the first puppy to the bitch and, if necessary, try to get them both sucking while you await the third puppy.

The rest of the litter
Subsequent arrivals should be dealt with in the same way. After the first few puppies, the bitch will soon get used to the routine and will cooperate with you. She may even decide that she can do the job perfectly well on her own. If so, let her do most of the work, but it is better not to allow her to tear at the cord as she may pull too hard, thereby causing the puppy an umbilical hernia.

She may well appreciate drinks at regular intervals during the whelping — either water or milk is ideal (this is one of the few instances when milk is a good idea). Another favourite drink is milky tea, with a little sugar.

You will need to keep an eye on the height of the intra-red lamp. This will need to be high enough so as not to overheat the bitch, but low enough to keep the puppies warm. During the whelping, it is better to meet the needs of the bitch rather than the puppies. If a puppy appears to be too cold, it can be placed in the incubator in order to warm it up.

If the bitch appears to be having difficulty in pushing out a puppy, it is often a good idea to take her for a short walk — the exercise will often start a puppy into motion down from the uterus. Always take an old towel with you and be ready to catch a puppy, if need be; many a puppy has been born this way. If it is dark, take a torch with you as well, so that you can see what is happening. This exercise will also encourage her to urinate, thereby further reducing internal pressure.

It may be of interest to weigh your puppies as they are born. This may also be useful for future reference and for comparison with any subsequent litters. Experienced breeders rarely weigh their puppies, preferring to use their experience to tell whether the puppies are normal

(the correct birth weight is generally about ¾-1¼ lb (325-550g).

You will also find it helpful to have pen and paper handy in order to note down the time of arrival of each puppy, its sex, colour, any interesting or unusual characteristics and whether the bitch has passed the placenta. The latter is important, as you must be sure that all the placentas have been expelled. Anything retained in the uterus is likely to cause problems later.

POST-WHELPING

The average litter size is about six to eight puppies. This is a convenient number for the bitch to manage and will give each puppy the maximum opportunity to feed as and when it needs to do so. Smaller litters of three or less are not uncommon. The largest litter I know of was 17, all of which were reared successfully.

Deciding when the last puppy has been born can sometimes be a problem. It is not unusual to think that the last one has arrived when there may be, in fact, one or even two more tucked up inside the uterus. Sometimes an examination of the bitch will enable you to feel that her flanks are hollow, with no puppy bulges in them. Often the bitch herself will indicate that she has finished by relaxing and settling down to rest and nurse her family.

The contractions may continue after what is believed to be the last puppy has been born. This may indicate that there is another puppy to come, or it may simply be the bitch attempting to expel a retained placenta or other debris. The bitch is likely to continue to discharge quite heavily for the first 24 hours after whelping. The discharge is normally dark bloody-red or brownish coloured liquid and is quite normal, so should not be the cause of any alarm. The precise amount of discharge can vary quite considerably. Some bitches lose very little both during or after the whelping and effectively dry up within the first 24 hours, while others will continue to have some discharge for several days.

The bitch may well continue to discharge slightly for anything up to six weeks after the whelping. Again, this is quite normal unless the discharge becomes a thick blackish or greenish-black viscous fluid, which indicates an infection in the uterus requiring immediate veterinary attention. A discharge of bright red blood indicates some damage to the uterus, again requiring medical help.

Bedding

It is best to keep newspaper in the whelping box for the first 24 hours as this can be changed easily as and when necessary. A small piece of blanket or an old towel should be placed under the puppies in order to enable them to grip when feeding; there is nothing worse than seeing tiny puppies sliding around on newspaper. The newspaper should then give way to a blanket or some other bedding material as soon as possible. There are several varieties of polyester

bedding marketed for use in the whelping box which are very effective, particularly as they are water-repellent, with any fluids soaking into a pad of newspaper which is placed underneath. These are not suitable in a kennel which has sawdust on the floor, as the sawdust tends to clog up the fibres and is very difficult to remove. A piece of old carpet also serves as a very effective form of bedding. It may be necessary to change the bedding if it becomes soiled, so spare supplies should be kept ready. Blankets and polyester bedding can be washed, though if they are badly soiled it is probably more hygienic to dispose of them.

There is one thing to beware of with blankets — or even polyester bedding. It is not unusual for a bitch to decide that she does not want any bedding in the whelping

Below: *'Judy' with her new family. She will feed her puppies exclusively for the first three weeks of their lives.*

box and to push it to one side. This creates the risk that puppies may be buried under the bedding or folds.

Suckling
Once you have got your bitch and her litter of puppies settled down, you will need to watch them carefully to ensure that they are all strong enough to push their way to the teats. For the first few days, you will need to check that the smaller or weaker puppies are obtaining their fair share of food. Usually, after about 48 hours they will have grown sufficiently strong to reach the teats themselves. At this early stage, each puppy takes a relatively small amount of milk at intervals of about 15 minutes, although they can survive for longer periods between feeds if necessary. Keep a careful watch on the infra red lamp over the puppies. This should be lowered to a height as close to the puppies as possible — usually just above the standing height of the bitch. If this makes the bitch too hot, it may be necessary to raise it for a while. The main objective is to keep the puppies warm.

It is very important that each puppy should get its fair share of the milk produced by the bitch during the first 48 hours of her lactation. This milk is known as colostrum. It is richer in protein and vitamins than the later milk, so gives the puppies a good start in life. It also contains antibodies which will give the puppies protection from disease. While some antibody protection is obtained from the bitch while in the uterus, the major part is obtained from the colostrum. Any puppy denied this colostrum is liable to be more prone to infection.

If you have a large litter, say over eight puppies, it is a good idea to divide the puppies into two halves. Give her one half to look after, and place the other half in the incubator for safety. Swap the puppies over about every 20 to 30 minutes. This will ensure that all the puppies get an equal chance of feeding and being cleaned up. It may only be

necessary to do this for the first 12 to 24 hours, as the puppies grow very quickly in size and strength once they start feeding. They soon develop a rhythm, so that once they are all in the whelping box together, some will be sleeping while others are feeding.

As soon as it is convenient to do so after the bitch has finished whelping, and certainly within the first 12 hours, you should ask your vet to visit your bitch.

Settling in
After the whelping has finished, the bitch is likely to be very tired and may even be completely exhausted, and simply want to sleep. The best advice is to let her. Ensure that the puppies stay close to her and that she lies full length on her side rather than curled in a tight ball, so that the puppies will be able to feed. Sometimes it is necessary to use a bit of persuasion at first, but they usually receive the message quite quickly. Some bitches, however, are very excited by the puppies and are almost wide awake. Discourage them from washing the puppies too much, particularly if it is a small litter, as this often results in the bitch rolling the puppies around the whelping box thereby unsettling them and preventing them from feeding.

A maiden bitch may not know what puppies are, and may nip the first one born. The maternal bond is very quickly established though, and this is rarely a long-term problem. It is advisable to make sure that the first puppy is safely delivered as it is not unknown for the first puppy to be eaten, still attached to the placenta. I have even seen a bitch frightened when the first puppy cried. It is therefore a good idea to tell her what a lovely baby she has got, encourage her to let it suck and persuade her to clean it up. Also, make sure that she does not chew or pull the ends of the cords. This can cause bleeding and even umbilical hernia.

For the first two weeks, the puppies cannot urinate or defaecate for themselves; they rely on the mother to lick them to stimulate these functions. Most bitches will do this instinctively, but you should make sure that she is doing so, and that she is attending to each puppy. If she is not, and you cannot persuade her to do so, you will have to do it yourself by gently stroking the appropriate parts of the puppies with a swab of cotton wool.

Some bitches have a wonderful nest sense and will always enter the whelping box carefully, sitting in a vacant space and very gently settling down around the puppies without hurting them. Other bitches are very clumsy, simply jumping in and dropping down among the puppies. Such bitches are very likely to sit on the puppies and damage or even kill them in the process, so you should gather the puppies into one part of the whelping box before letting her get in, and then encourage her to do it carefully.

Put the puppies back alongside her teats once she is lying down. Hopefully, this procedure will teach her nest sense, as well as protecting the puppies from harm.

As soon as the bitch has started to dry up after about 24 hours, it is a good idea to wash her back end with warm water and some dog shampoo in order to remove the blood from her coat. This will not only make her feel much more comfortable and keep the bedding clean but will prevent an excessive loss of coat, which is likely to occur if the blood is not removed.

Food and drink
For the first week, the bitch will probably go off her food and show little desire to eat anything. This is quite normal, though some bitches do not seem to be affected in this way. Keep tempting her to eat by offering interesting food, but do not force her to eat if she is not ready to do so. It is much more important to keep her drinking. Water should always be available on demand. Milk is always acceptable, but it is not wise to give unlimited quantities. Milky tea with a little sugar is often an acceptable alternative. Egg custard is very nutritious, as is rice pudding.

Below: *As the puppies get older, the bitch will tend to leave them for longer periods of time, generally to sleep.*

Chicken or oxtail soup are also good standbys, either as a drink or poured over the food. At first, she may prefer them as a drink with a small amount of meat or bread soaked in them. The amount of fluid that you will need to give the bitch will increase as the puppies grow older and their demand for milk becomes greater.

WHELPING PROBLEMS

Dobermanns normally whelp easily, with few problems. Even so, it is as well to be aware of some of the potential problems with which you may be faced.

Bitches may appear to be in whelp at about four to five weeks after mating, but then all the abdominal enlargement disappears. This may simply be a false pregnancy, or the bitch may have aborted the puppies. Even if you think that the bitch has lost her litter, or indeed that she has not conceived at all, it is always worth keeping an open mind until the due date has passed.

Resuscitation
If a puppy appears to be dead when it is born it is always worth attempting to resuscitate it, as such puppies can often be saved. Lay the puppy on its back in your hands and give mouth-to-mouth resuscitation. To do this, open its mouth and blow air into it in order to push air into the lungs. This is sometimes sufficient to expand the lungs and start the puppy breathing. Make sure that you wipe any fluid or mucous out of the mouth and nostrils as normal in order to avoid blowing fluid into the lungs. If this does not work, bend the puppy inwards, thereby expelling the air from the lungs, then open the puppy out again, thereby forcing air back into the lungs. It may be necessary to continue this operation for as long as five or even 10 minutes before life returns to the puppy and it begins to cry and breath independently. Unfortunately not every puppy can be resuscitated,

but enough are revived to make the effort worthwhile.

Defects
You may sometimes find a defective puppy. The faults may include a cleft palate, which is relatively easy to see — when the puppy sucks milk it will flow into the nose and drip out of the nostrils. Puppies are occasionally born with a hare-lip or with the intestines growing outside the body. With obvious defects such as these, the puppy is not viable and should be culled.

Some defects do not manifest themselves until the puppies are older, but if the defect is such as to prevent the puppy growing into a normal dog it is again better to cull them as early as possible. Squealers occasionally occur, though I suspect this is a hereditary defect rather than one which occurs at random. Squealers are unable to get off their backs and when placed on their feet will tend to move round in a circular manner and roll on to their backs again. This is accompanied by a characteristic crying. The problem is caused by a defect in the ear which affects the balance. Such puppies do not improve if reared and their constant crying unsettles the bitch, so they should be culled as soon as the defect becomes obvious.

Other defects may not become evident until the puppies are several weeks old. Deafness is one example. This is normally only detected when the puppy does not respond to activities around it and it is surprising how long this fault can remain unobserved, since the puppy will react to the movements of its siblings. Whilst a deaf puppy will grow up otherwise normally there may be problems in later life, as the dog will lack one of its main awareness sensors. There is also the possibility that it may be a hereditary factor which should not be perpetuated. Hard though it may be, such puppies should be quietly destroyed.

Whether or not to cull some of the puppies in a large litter is often the subject of debate. Personally I am not in favour of culling unless there is something wrong with the puppies.

It is not unusual for a litter to contain one small puppy which does not grow. As the other puppies grow, the little one tends to stay much the same size, so getting proportionately smaller. Such puppies are often not viable, having some internal defect, and will simply fade away by about the second week. Do not let such things upset you — there is nothing you can do to help them, and you will have to learn to accept the occasional failure.

Eclampsia

One problem which you should always be on the look-out for is eclampsia, also known as milk fever. This is caused by a drop in the blood calcium level as a result of the milk being drawn off by the puppies and the bitch's body being unable to replace it sufficiently quickly. The symptoms to watch for are quite characteristic; the bitch will appear restless, hot and panting and will have a staggering movement, which is due to muscle spasms caused by the lack of calcium. Once you have satisfied yourself that it is not simply because the bitch is too hot, you should always suspect that it is eclampsia. Contact your vet immediately, as this is an emergency situation in which urgent attention is required. The vet will give the bitch an injection of calcium, which will result in the symptoms disappearing within 20 minutes. If eclampsia is not treated the symptoms will get steadily worse and the bitch will have convulsions, lapse into unconsciousness and eventually die. In my experience, the usual time for Dobermanns to suffer from eclampsia is within the first four days after whelping, though it is possible for it to occur after this time. It is also possible for the bitch to suffer from eclampsia on more than one occasion, so do not assume that once treated the

problem will go away. The use of liquid calcium after whelping, appears to be helpful in reducing eclampsia.

Mastitis

If the milk is not drawn off from every teat, it is possible for milk to collect and form hard lumps at the base of one or more teats. This is described as mastitis. Check the bitch's teats each day to ensure that they are soft and supple. If you detect mastitis, try to persuade the puppies to suck from the affected teats, thereby drawing off the milk. It is also advisable for the bitch to receive an injection from the vet to help overcome the problem. Mastitis normally occurs where there is a small litter which only suck from the lower teats or where the bitch tends to lie on one elbow, thereby masking one or more teats from the puppies.

Insufficient milk

You may occasionally find that the bitch does not have sufficient milk. Puppies which suck then fall asleep can be assumed to be obtaining enough milk, but be suspicious if they are restless, cry a lot and move from teat to teat sucking at each for only a few minutes. If the bitch is short of milk, increase her fluid intake and the protein content of her diet. Alternatively, check that she is not unwell. This is one time when it is useful to take her temperature as a guide. If this is more than about two degrees higher than the normal 101.2°F (38.4°C) you should seek veterinary advice.

If you need to supplement the milk intake of the puppies you should not use cow's milk as both the protein and fat content are too low. Goat's milk has a higher protein content, though still not as high as bitch's milk. However, goat's milk is often used with great success and I know of many litters of puppies which have been hand-reared from birth on nothing else. Alternatively, you could use a proprietary brand of milk substitute designed specifically for rearing puppies. This will usually be in the form of a powder which will need to be reconstituted with water according to the manufacturer's instructions. These milk substitutes will have a protein and fat content similar to that in bitch's milk. It is a good idea to obtain a purpose-made feeding bottle, available from your vet, in case you need to hand feed the puppies. Failing that, a small baby's bottle with a soft teat will do. Always ensure that it is properly cleaned after each use.

If the bitch is particularly awkward, has no milk or is ill, then it may be worth considering removing the puppies from her and hand-rearing them. They will need feeding at regular intervals, though the intervals can be increased as they grow bigger. At birth, they will want feeding at least every 30 minutes, but by two weeks old they should be able to go for up to three hours between feeds.

If you are leaving the intervals too long, they will quickly tell you. Before deciding that the bitch does not have enough milk, however, remember that in the first few days the puppies take only relatively small amounts of milk and that the milk flow will increase as the demand from the puppies increases. It is always best to let the bitch provide the milk whenever possible as hand-rearing is, at best, a poor substitute.

Another option is fostering. This is not often possible, however, as it does require another bitch which is not only lactating, but is willing to accept the puppies. The intended foster mum may herself have a litter but have sufficient milk to take on a few additional puppies.

Umbilical hernia
An umbilical hernia is a weak point in the abdominal wall. They may be caused by excessive pulling by the bitch at birth, but are more likely to be due to a hereditary factor. Small ones are rarely a problem, as they tend to disappear as the puppy grows. Larger ones will need attention, as it is possible for a section of the intestine to become

pinched in the hernia, thereby causing peritonitis. These should be surgically corrected once the puppy reaches 12 weeks of age and is old enough to withstand the anaesthetic. It is only a superficial operation and recovery is quick.

Protracted labour
There may be occasions when a bitch appears unable to pass a puppy. This may be before any puppies have arrived or during the whelping and may be due to a number of possible reasons. The puppy may be unusually large, or be lying at an awkward angle or caught up with the cord or the placenta. Alternatively, it may be dead. The problem may be with the bitch — uterine inertia, a stricture of the cervix, or simply exhaustion or lack of muscle tone. It could be due to there only being a few puppies, so resulting in very little internal pressure.

Whatever the reason, it is always difficult to know when to be patient and let the puppy come in its own time and when the bitch really does need help. Where the bitch shows no apparent signs of starting to whelp, it is best not to interfere until she is about 48 hours overdue, as the puppies are still likely to be alive, provided the delay is not due to some other problem. After 48 hours, it is advisable to discuss what action should be taken with your vet.If she is contracting, is obviously in some distress and is unable to pass the first puppy, you will need to take action quickly.

While some bitches produce at regular 20-minute intervals, it is not unusual for there to be periods of three or four hours between puppies. The bitch will usually be resting in these long intervals. If she continues contracting and straining hard for any length of time, it may be an indication of trouble. It is probably better to err on the side of caution and seek veterinary help too early rather than too late. A puppy which takes too long to be expelled may be born dead but, even worse, it will hold back any remaining puppies.

Chapter Two

THE FIRST WEEKS

WHELPING TO WEANING

The bitch will feed the puppies for the first three weeks, so during this time your main concern will be to ensure that she has sufficient food and drink to enable her to generate the milk needed to feed them.

Once she has begun eating normally again, usually after 7-10 days, the bitch should be fed two meals per day. She will require anything up to 2½ lb (1.1kg) food at each meal, though the precise amount will vary from bitch to bitch. The food should be nutritional and contain up to 30 per cent protein. This should be supplemented by drinks of milk, soup or tea at regular intervals. Water should continue to be available at all times. Discontinue giving the liquid calcium after about 10 days, and instead add a tablespoonful of calcium powder to the food each day.

The bitch will be reluctant to leave the puppies for any reason for about the first five days. It may therefore be necessary to feed her in the whelping box. Do not leave the food in the box when you move out of the room, as many bitches will guard the food, whether or not they actually want it, even from their own puppies. It is often necessary to remove the puppies to the incubator in order to persuade the bitch to get out of the whelping

box. Once out, she should be taken outside for toilet purposes. Over the next 10 days the bitch will gradually become more willing to leave the puppies for short periods. After this, she may well spend more time away from the puppies than with them and you may even need to force her to feed them.

During the first three weeks you should see a steady increase in the size of the puppies and they should show a steady gain in weight. This will inevitably vary from litter to litter and even from puppy to puppy, but as a rough guide, they should increase from about 15oz (420g) birth-weight to 3½ lb (1.5kg) at 3 weeks. The eyes will open at about 10 days, though they will not be functional until about 2½ weeks. Similarly, the ears will gradually open and will begin to function at about the same time. The sense of smell is probably well developed at a much earlier age, since they always appear to be able to move towards the bitch and are able to identify the teats almost from the moment of birth.

You should clip the puppies' toenails every few days as they grow quite long and are very sharp. If they are not cut they will scratch the bitch's underside, which will not only make her sore but may make her less willing to feed the puppies. This should be done with a pair of blunt-ended scissors. Place one blade of the scissors under the nail and slide it along until it is caught by the overhanging hooked end. Snip this overhanging part of the nail off, but do not remove more or you may cut the quick.

If the bitch's underside does become sore, possibly from the puppies' nails, it is helpful to rub in some hand cream or antiseptic cream, or even plain petroleum jelly. Do not use anything which could be harmful to the bitch or the puppies if licked.

Docking

Now that docking is optional in the British breed standard, breeders in the UK may not wish to dock the tails. While a breeder has always had the right to leave tails undocked it was rarely done until recently, since it was contrary to the requirements of the breed standard. However, the Dobermann is widely recognized as a docked breed, and before deciding not to dock you will need to consider carefully whether you would be able to sell the puppies if they are undocked. While docking is an emotive issue, I consider that the Dobermann is still a docked breed and would like to think that it will continue to be so, since the short length of tail is one of the main features and gives the breed its classical symmetry, its elegance and its instant recognition.

Docking is generally done on the third day although if the puppies are very small, they may be left to the fourth day. The breed standard suggests that the tail should be docked at the first or second joint. I prefer the tail to be docked at the second or third joint, thereby giving a long enough length of tail to give that balanced look to the dog. For this reason, I consider that a first-joint dock is too short.

It is quite legal for anyone over the age of 18 years to dock tails provided it is done before the puppy's eyes are open. Unless you have had some experience at docking tails or have been shown

---

Below: *As the puppies grow, the sharp points of the toe nails should be carefully cut off every few days for safety.*

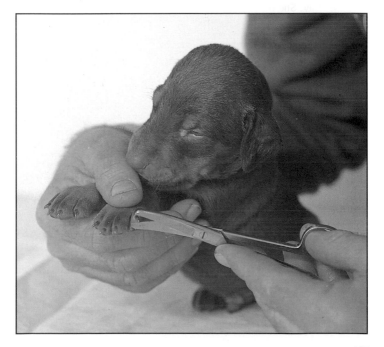

how to do it properly, you would be well advised not to attempt to do it yourself. Either arrange for your vet to do it for you, and accept that he will almost certainly cut them, or ask an experienced breeder to do them for you.

Dew claws

Dew claws, which correspond to the human thumb, normally occur on only the front legs. These should be removed at the same time as the tails are docked, not only because the breed standard requires this to be done, but because retained dew claws are often damaged, causing painful injuries. Like tail docking, the removal of dew claws should be left either to a vet or to an experienced breeder.

WEANING

Once the puppies are three weeks old, they will be sufficiently developed to be able to digest food other than milk. By now, they will be demanding ever-increasing quantities of milk from the bitch

which in all probability she cannot provide. She will also be losing the strong maternal bond and will be less inclined to feed them, particularly as the milk teeth will now be coming through.

At three weeks, therefore, it is necessary to start to wean the puppies. This generally takes about two weeks, which is effectively a transition period during which they eat what they can but rely on the bitch to supplement their feeding. By about five weeks old, they should be eating sufficient food not to rely on the bitch, though she may still be willing to allow them to suck. The amount of food she provides by this stage is gradually declining.

At about this age the puppies also begin to become mobile, so you should remove the front of the box, thereby allowing them out on

Below: *At three weeks, the puppies should be taught to be bed-clean. Paper in the whelping box will help with this.*

to the floor. For the first few days, you should put them on to the floor whenever they wake up or you disturb them in order for them to learn to be bed-clean. They will soon get the idea, and once they have performed they can be put back into the box. After a day or two, they will learn to find their own way back into bed. Until you are sure that they can all do this you should box them in at night, so as to avoid risking a puppy being stranded and catching a chill.

Even when they can go in and out of the box themselves, you will need to continue the toilet training. During this period it is better to remove the blanket and put newspaper in the box, as this can be replaced as necessary. A small area of blanket or a carpet square can be placed in one corner of the box to give them something soft on which to sleep. This bed-training generally takes about one week, but once they are bed-clean the paper can be dispensed with and normal bedding used again.

If you are rearing the puppies in a kennel or an outside building it is a good idea to put sawdust on the floor as it is easy to obtain and can be swept and disposed of as necessary. It also leaves the kennel floor dry. Make sure that the sawdust comes from a timber merchant and is clean and dry. Avoid sawdust that is too fine or is from a workshop where the timber is treated with chemicals.

If you are rearing the puppies in the house, you may prefer to put newspaper on the floor. However, once they get beyond four weeks of age they can make a considerable mess and it may be better to transfer them to an outside kennel, shed or garage, if you have suitable facilities. Whatever accommodation is used will need to be kept warm — certainly up to about 60°F (15°C). The overhead infra-red heater should also be retained. If the litter is being reared in the summer it may be possible to do without heating during the day, though the infra-red heater should be switched on at night. You will

need to exercise your discretion, with the weather determining the level of heating that you need to provide. If the temperature is particularly hot, you may need to consider means of keeping the puppies cool.

Weaning puppies can be very frustrating, as they are sometimes reluctant to take food for themselves. You may also find yourself preparing meals which they do not eat. This must be accepted philosophically. However, the bitch is likely to consider it her duty to clean up any food that the puppies leave; at least this ensures that it is not entirely wasted.

Every breeder has his own idea of how to wean and rear puppies and whatever method is adopted, they all seem to manage quite successfully. This suggests that there is no such thing as a right way or a wrong way, so long as the puppies are given an adequate amount of good-quality food at regular intervals.

The first meal

The best food for the first meal at three weeks of age is raw meat. You should use top-quality stewing beef and either scrape it or cut it very finely. Alternatively, use top-quality mince (chopped beef) that does not contain too much fat. When preparing this meal, make one pile of meat for each puppy, with any offcuts going to the bitch. It is difficult to be precise as to how much each puppy will take but about 2 – 3oz (50-75g) would be a reasonable estimate. The puppies should be fed individually to ensure that they each get their fair share. Place the puppy on your lap or on a table top, making sure that it does not fall off, and hold one portion of meat under its nose. The smell of the meat alone will often be enough to get the puppy eating. Alternatively, push a small amount of meat into its mouth in order for it to get the taste. It rarely takes very long before the meat is consumed, though it may well be that not every puppy will eat its share. This does not matter, as you cannot

push them faster than their rate of development allows. Do not let the puppy gulp too much meat down in one mouthful — make it swallow a little bit before allowing it to take the next mouthful. It is very easy for a puppy to take more than it can swallow and get the meat stuck in the back of its throat. It is also a wise precaution to keep your artery forceps handy, so that if this should happen you can pull the meat out from the back of the throat again. As each puppy is fed it should be separated from those awaiting feeding so that you know which ones have or have not eaten. One meal of raw meat will be sufficient for the first two days of weaning. It is better to give them the meat in the evening, as they will sleep through the night on a full stomach.

The third day
By the third day, the puppies should be sufficiently advanced to eat two meals per day. Give them some egg custard in the morning in addition to the raw meat in the evening. Again, it is better to feed the puppies individually so you can ensure that each one is given every opportunity to learn to eat. Put some egg custard in a small dish and hold the puppy securely in one

Above: *Weaning should start at about three weeks. The first meals should be finely chopped raw meat and egg custard.*

hand and the dish in the other. If the puppies are very advanced or very hungry they will quickly discover that you are offering them food. Occasionally you will meet with obstinate resistance. If so, don't worry — simply try again the next day. It sometimes helps to gently touch the puppy's nose to the surface of the egg custard, as the puppy then licks its nose and mouth and tastes it. Egg custard is very easy to make. Simply beat up two eggs to one pint of milk in a metal jug, then stand it in a saucepan containing water to a depth of about two inches. Bring to the boil, cover and simmer for five minutes, then leave in the hot water for a further five minutes.

Egg custard is a particularly good starter food as it is very nutritional and as it is semi-solid the puppies are able to suck it off the plate. It is thus a useful transition between sucking and eating. An alternative to egg custard is chicken soup. This is readily available in cans, so is a convenient form of food. It is best fed warm or cold rather than hot.

The fifth day

By the fifth day the puppies should be sufficiently advanced to be eating a reasonable amount of each meal that they are offered. The raw meat can now be discontinued and the number of meals increased to three, preferably spaced out at fairly regular intervals throughout the day. At this stage the food can be put into a large dish for communal feeding. This has the added advantage that one puppy feeding will entice the others to eat as well. This can be a very messy period, as they will walk in the food, spread it all over each other and even fall into it. The best thing to do is leave them to it for a while then return with the bitch, who will generally take great delight in cleaning up the dish and then the puppies.

Egg custard and chicken soup are still useful meals but by now some bread should be broken up into the soup (if the puppies progress fast, then bread can be added earlier). The precise amount depends upon the number of puppies and how much they are able to eat. This will very quickly become evident by trial and error. You should aim to get the puppies on to three meals per day by four weeks of age. Many breeders advocate giving the puppies up to five meals per day for the first few weeks. In my experience this is too many, as the puppies are not able to digest one meal properly before the next one arrives. This three meals per day regime should continue until the puppies are sold at 8 to 12 weeks of age.

The seventh day

By the seventh day, i.e. at four weeks of age, you should be adding some complete food to the soup rather than bread. This will be more nutritional and provide additional bulk, but will still be very largely a drink as well as a feed. Alternatively, you could introduce them to a meat/biscuit or meat/complete food meal. Rabbit is particularly useful, as most puppies cannot resist it. The easiest way to

prepare the rabbit is to cook it thoroughly in a pressure cooker. It is a tedious job cleaning the meat off the bones but it is worth the effort, as it is invariably enjoyed by the puppies. Cut the meat into small pieces, add some of the gravy and soak bread or a small amount of complete food in it. One rabbit will generally provide several meals. Other meat can be used if preferred, but it must be fresh and neither too fat nor too rich. At this stage it is better to avoid houndmeal or biscuit meal, as it may be too rough for them, even when soaked. It is also advisable to avoid tinned dog meat and raw milk, as these are likely to result in the puppies developing diarrhoea.

There is an infinite variety of other foods that can be given during this first week of weaning. These include macaroni cheese and rice pudding, both of which are easily obtainable in tins. Scrambled egg is usually very welcome. Many breeders consider cottage cheese to be a very useful early feed. The common factor in most of these foods is that they are high protein, easily digested and provide both fluid and food.

Four to five weeks

Between the ages of four and five weeks the aim should be to consolidate the three meals per day procedure, with the main meals being given morning and evening, with a lighter, milk-based meal at midday. At this stage, one of the better quality precooked complete feeds is best, as it provides a carefully balanced diet and is easy to prepare. Ideally, you should use a high protein (about 27 per cent) puppy grade. This should be soaked with hot water before use. Initially, it should be made very sloppy by the addition of a small amount of milk, chicken soup or gravy. The latter can be made by mashing a tin of dog meat with hot water — the meat gravy so produced can be poured over the surface of the food. The amount of meat will depend on the number of puppies being fed, but it is better to use it sparingly. As the puppies get a few days older, they will be able to cope with the normally soaked food. Chicken or oxtail soup poured over the dinner will certainly make the food more appetizing and will encourage them to eat — if they need any encouragement.

During this weaning stage it is advisable to give the puppies a few drops of liquid vitamins each day. The vitamin drops should contain vitamins A, B, C and D, and should be given until the puppies are established on a well-balanced diet at about five weeks. Estimate about one drop per puppy each day. One of the advantages of using one of the complete feeds is that they not only contain a balanced diet, but also all the necessary vitamins and minerals.

By about four weeks of age, a bowl of water should be provided for the puppies. It is surprising how quickly they learn to drink water. The bowl should be heavy and broad-based, so as to prevent it being tipped over. The water will need to be changed at frequent intervals.

By this time the puppies will be becoming aware of their surroundings and will begin to react to your approach. It is fascinating to notice how their development progresses day by day. At this age, you should begin (or continue) to handle them and talk to them. Apart from being one of the most enjoyable aspects of having puppies, this early socialization is very important, as it gets them used to people. They should also learn to accept being away from people for periods of time. A radio playing in the background will help them to get used to everyday sounds of life and will give them the feeling of human company.

Feeding the bitch

Continue to give the bitch plenty of food and drink over this two-week weaning period. She should now be eating two meals per day in order to begin the long road back to peak condition. As a rough guide, she should be offered up to 2½lb

(1.1kg) prepared weight of food both morning and evening. This will clearly need to be reduced if the bitch has managed to come through without noticeable loss of body or condition. Water should still always be available, and other drinks given more sparingly — ½pt (300ml) milk or 1lb (450g) rice pudding will probably be adequate. While she will still be feeding the puppies to some extent, they should be relying on her less and less and you should be thinking about drying up her milk supply. A gradual reduction in her fluid intake, rather than a sudden withdrawal, is the best procedure.

WEANING TO SELLING

From five weeks onwards, continue feeding three meals per day. At this stage, the two main meals can either be meat and biscuit or a complete food. If you are using meat and biscuit, the meat should be lightly boiled. The gravy can be used to soak the biscuit meal. This should be a puppy grade meal until the puppies are about 12 weeks old, after which they will be big enough to cope with a terrier grade, which is slightly larger. Aim for a balanced diet of about one third meat and two thirds biscuit. Increase the quantity of food as the puppies get bigger — the best way to find out how much they need is by trial and error. Leave the food with them for a while, and adjust the quantity given at the next meal. As a rough guide, allow about 1lb (450g) prepared food per puppy per meal at about six weeks of age. Don't be alarmed if the puppies look bloated — they will soon sleep it off and be back for more.

Worming

As soon as the puppies are eating properly at about 3½-4 weeks of age, they should be wormed in order to remove roundworms from the gut. Some puppies can be heavily infested and if they are not removed the worms can block the intestines or bore through the intestine wall, or cause respiratory

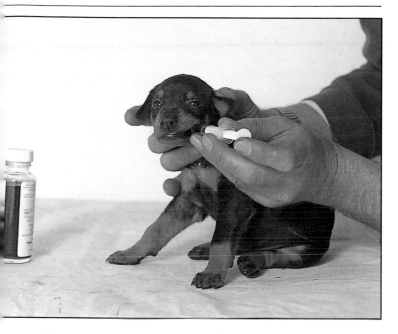

Above: *For the first worming, use a plastic syringe (without needle) to give a chocolate-flavoured liquid wormer.*

problems. In extreme cases this can be fatal. Once these worms have been removed the puppies will thrive more rapidly, as they will then derive all the benefit from their food. Apart from the obvious benefit to the puppies you also have a social duty to worm them, so as to minimize the risk of the worms or worm eggs getting into the environment.

For the first worming, I suggest using a liquid worming solution using piperazine citrate. This should be given immediately prior to a meal. The dose should be about 1ml and is best squirted into the mouth from a disposable plastic syringe (without the needle). Do not overdose, as this can be harmful; it is better to give a second dose a few days later. Care will need to be taken to ensure that you worm each puppy only once and that none are missed. The advantage of this type of wormer is that it is palatable, and being a liquid, is more likely to make the desired contact with the worms. Piperazine citrate is also good because it expels the worms some 12 hours later, rather than dissolving them, as do certain other

wormers. This enables you to remove the worms for disposal. This is important, as the puppies should be wormed again at about five weeks and six weeks old. For these later wormings, use piperazine citrate in either powder or tablet form. As the bitch will have cleaned up after the puppies, she will almost certainly have re-infested herself with worms. She should therefore also be wormed.

It is not unusual for the puppies to develop diarrhoea between three and six weeks, though they are otherwise fit and healthy. This may be due to milk, milk products such as rice pudding, the changes in diet or even the effects of worming. If left untreated, the problem may resolve itself without any intervention. If it persists, or you feel that some treatment should be given, use neomycin drops. Give each affected puppy a few drops, using a pipette or a disposable syringe (without the needle).

Above: *Having bred your litter and reared your puppies in good health, you must make sure that they go to good homes.*

Consult your vet as to the appropriate dose as this will vary according to the individual proprietary brand. Alternatively, obtain an electrolyte powder from your vet and sprinkle a small amount over the dinner — say, one teaspoonful per dose to cover the whole litter. This will help to dry up the puppies.

Handling
Continue to handle your puppies as often as you can, and try to get them used to the normal household noises and activities. This will prevent them from being frightened by such things when they are confronted by them in later life. Do not allow all your friends to handle them, however, as there is always the risk that they will introduce some infectiion to the puppies. This is particularly important if they also have dogs. It is not simply that their dogs may be unhealthy, but that there is the risk of cross-infection.

Dobermann puppies may well start fighting amongst themselves from about seven weeks of age. While the males are likely to be the worst, the bitches can be just as bad. If necessary, you should be prepared to separate them into mixed-sex pairs. It is not a good idea to give them toys to play with unless you are on hand to supervise their games. Toys will certainly occupy them, but can also be the bone of contention that starts trouble.

Examine the puppies carefully at regular intervals. Make sure that they are not chewing each others' tails. Occasionally a male puppy will have his penis chewed, which can cause problems. In instances such as these the affected puppy should be isolated and, in bad cases, treated with penicillin and antiseptic ointment.

The bitch will generally retain an

interest in the puppies until about seven weeks old. After this, she will merely want to check that you are looking after them properly. The bitch should be allowed regular access to them between three and seven weeks of age. Her milk supply will begin to dry up after about four weeks. If she continues to produce after this, it is a good idea to let the puppies drain her once a day, but you should also try to dry her up as well by reducing her fluid intake and, if necessary, by giving her antihistamine, which will dry up her secretions very quickly. Your vet will advise you as to the appropriate treatment. Most bitches will regain their tuck-up after the first litter and some will manage it after the second. Otherwise, you should be prepared to accept that yours may never regain her maiden figure.

SELLING

Selling the puppies can be one of the hardest parts of breeding. It is very easy to form strong emotional ties with them to the point where the thought of selling them seems like selling the children. However, when you sell a puppy to its new owner you are giving that puppy the opportunity of having its own home and developing its own individual personality.

Do not let the puppies go until they are at least seven weeks of age — ideally, you should keep them until they are eight weeks old. At this age, they will be big and strong enough to lead an independent existence. They will also have been wormed several times and will be established on three meals per day.

Do not inoculate your puppies before you sell them. They should still retain sufficient antibody protection from the mother, so it is by no means certain that any inoculation would actually be effective. If you have unsold puppies when they reach 12 weeks old, then these should be inoculated. You will be perfectly entitled to recoup the cost from the eventual purchaser.

Charge a fair price for your puppies — ask around if you are not sure what the normal going rate is. Do remember, though, that you may not be able to command the same price as the established and well-known breeders, even if your stock is as good as theirs. It is sometimes better to ask an average price and sell the puppies quickly than to hold out for a higher price and have to keep them for much longer. The increasing popularity of the breed means that more people are breeding puppies and any would-be purchaser therefore has a wider choice. It would only take a slight fall-off in demand or even a levelling-off, and it could well be that the supply of puppies would exceed the demand. It is therefore very important before you breed a litter of puppies to ensure that you really will be able to sell them. It also means that you will need to rear your puppies as well as possible — they should be fat, sleek and healthy-looking. A purchaser will be put off very quickly if the puppies are thin, look unhealthy, have spots on them or are housed in unclean or unattractive surroundings. As with any other consumer product, presentation is very important.

You will almost certainly need to advertise your puppies in order to attract customers. Advertisements can be placed in local papers or in the specialist canine press. Word of mouth can also help, so tell people that you have puppies to sell. When advertising, do it honestly. Make the puppies sound interesting but do not make false claims, such as 'certain winner', since you have no way of knowing the future potential of a puppy at such a young age.

Choosing the new home
Vet your potential customers carefully. Ask them why they want a Dobermann. It may well be that a Dobermann is not the right breed for them, or that they know nothing about them. Check that there will be someone at home to look after the puppy; it is not advisable to sell

a puppy to a family where all the members of the household are out all day. The puppy would not receive the necessary supervision and feeding, would likely to become neurotic through lack of human contact, noisy (so creating bad relationships with neighbours), destructive through boredom, and dirty through not being able to go out for toilet purposes when necessary.

Such a family may be better acquiring an older dog, possibly from Dobermann Rescue, which may adapt more easily to this kind of home and lifestyle. Even here, though, it is not an ideal set-up for an active breed of dog.

Below: *Owning a young Dobermann for the first time brings many new responsibilities. Your breeder can help you with advice.*

breed of dog such as a Dobermann.

Check that the prospective owners live in a property with access to a garden which is properly fenced in. Do not sell puppies to people living in high-rise apartments — this is courting disaster. Never sell a male puppy to a household which already has a male dog of any breed and certainly never sell two male puppies to anyone, as sooner or later they will fight and you or Dobermann Rescue will be asked to take one of them back to find it a new home. This is distressing for all involved, especially the dog. This checking out of potential customers is vital, as the future well-being of your puppies is in your hands. You owe it to them to ensure that they go to loving and caring homes. If you have any doubts about a potential home, say no. It may be

embarrassing at the time, but the peace of mind it gives you afterwards will make it worthwhile.

Documentation
Always give the purchaser all the documents relating to the puppy. These should include a signed pedigree; the Kennel Club registration certificate with a signed Kennel Club transfer of ownership (or, alternatively, a partially completed registration form, obtainable from your national Kennel Club, which will enable them to register their own puppy); a diet sheet, which should give sufficient details of how the puppy is being fed to enable the new owners to continue the same way, or at least to change to their own methods gradually. The diet sheet should also contain details of worming and any other relevant

information that a new owner might need — remember, they may never have owned or looked after a dog before. You should also give a receipt for the money which will also be a useful record of the sales for your own use, and a temporary insurance cover with one of the specialist canine insurance companies, even if you ask the new owners to pay the cost. This will enable them to recoup the cost of the puppy in the unfortunate event of it dying or being lost within the first months. There may also be some recompense in respect of certain other eventualities. Sensible owners will extend their temporary cover to a full policy, including third party cover.

Impress upon the new owners that you will always be willing to give them any help and advice they need, even if it means your having to seek advice from others first. This is part of your responsibility.

Problems
The purchaser who changes his mind after he has bought the puppy can cause problems. It can be risky putting such a puppy back with the remainder of the litter, since it may introduce infection to which it has been exposed to your puppies. It may be prudent to ask them to keep it until it has been fully inoculated before you will take it back. As regards refunding the money, I consider this to be something to be agreed between the parties, depending on the individual circumstances. As a rule, I think that as the purchaser has changed his mind, he should not be entitled to expect his money back in full, and certainly not until you have resold the puppy. How long this takes will determine what percentage of the purchase price you refund. If the puppy is returned because it is defective in some way, then you have a much greater duty to give restitution, either financial or in the form of an alternative puppy. This is a complex area and one in which there are many legal points that will need to be considered should the need arise.

Appendix

Dobermann Clubs
Some Breed Clubs in Britain
Dobermann Club:
Mrs C. Wright, Woodview, 41 Gill Bank Road, Ilkey, W. Yorks LS29 0AU
Birmingham and District Dobermann Club:
Mr P.B. Rock, Otherton House, Penkridge, Staffs ST19 5NX Midland Dobermann Club:
Mrs M. Thompson, 25 Heather Avenue, Heath, Chesterfield, Derbyshire S44 5RF
North of England Dobermann Club:
Mr D. Brown, 48 Park Avenue, Sale, Cheshire M33 1HE
Scottish Dobermann Club:
Mr E. Neilson, Edcath Kennels, Bathgate, West Lothian South East England Dobermann Club:
Mrs M. Barton, Mill Cottage, Linfold Bridge, Kirdford, West Sussex
South West Dobermann Club:
Mrs G.A. Pascoe, Trevannick House, Wellington Plantation, Feock, Truro, Cornwall TR3 6QP
Welsh Dobermann Club:
Mrs B. Scandrett, 44 Fontygary Road, Rhoose, South Glamorgan

Some Doberman Pinscher Clubs in the United States
Doberman Pinscher Club of America: Corresp Sec, Ms Socorro C. Armstrong, 22371 Sequoia Circle, Lake Elsinoie, CA. 92330 Doberman Pinscher Club of Northern California: Ellen Hanley, 2874 Miranda Avenue, Alamo, CA 94507
Doberman Pinscher Club of Florida Inc: Donna Blackburn, 19810 N.E. 12th Avenue, North Miami, Florida 33179
Doberman Pinscher Club of Indiana: Linda S. Ambroz, 1836 W. 51st Street, Indianapolis, In 46208
Doberman Pinscher Club of Connecticut — New York:
Mary Manning, 14-11 155th Street, Beechurst, NY 11357
Doberman Pinscher Club of Western Pennsylvania: Ms May Keoppi, 103 Whitehill Circle, Pittsburgh, PA 15227

Abbreviations
AKC	American Kennel Club
ANKC	Australian National Kennel Club
AOC	Any other colour
B	Bitch
BIS	Best in Show
BOB	Best of Breed
BOS	Best Opposite Sex
CAC	Certificate dápitude au Championnat de Beauté
CACIB	Certificat d'apitude au Championnat International de Beauté
CD	Companion Dog
CDEX	Companion Dog Excellent
Ch	Champion
CKC	Canadian Kennel Club
D	Dog
FCI	Federation Cynologique Internationale
Int Ch	International Champion
JW	Junior Warrant
KC	Kennel Club (UK)
LKA	Ladies Kennel Association
LOF	Livre des Origines Francais (French Stud Book)

Magazines
The United Kingdom
The Kennel Gazette, 1-5 Clarges Street, Piccadilly, London W1Y 8AB.
Dog World, 9 Tufton Street, Ashford, Kent TN23 1QN.
Our Dogs, Oxford Road, Station Approach, Manchester.
Dogs Monthly, Unit One, Bowen Industrial Estate, Aberbargoed, Bargoed, Mid-Glamorgan, CF8 9ET.

The United States
Dog World Magazine, 300 West Adams Street, Chicago, Il 60606.
Pure-Bred Dogs/American Kennel Gazette, 51 Madison Avenue, New York, NY 10010.

Useful Addresses
Kennel Clubs
Australia Australian National Kennel Council, Royal Show Grounds, Ascot Vale, Victoria
Belgium Societe Royale Saint-Hubert, Avenue de l'Armee 25, B-1040, Brussels
Canada Canadian Kennel Club, 2150 Bloor Street West, Toronto M6S 1M8, Ontario
France Societe Centrale Canine, 215 Rue St Denis, 75083 Paris, Cedex 02
Germany Verband ffur das Deutsche Hundewesen (VDH), Postfach 1390, 46 Dortmund
Holland Raad van Beheer op Kynologisch Gebied in Nederland, Emmalaan 16, Amsterdam, Z
Ireland Irish Kennel Club, 23 Earlsfort Terrace, Dublin 2
Italy Ente Nazionale Della Cinofilia Italiana, Viale Premuda, 21 Milan
New Zealand New Zealand Kennel Club, Private Bag, Porirua, New Zealand
Spain Real Sociedad Central de Fomento de las razas en Espana, Los Madrazo 20, Madrid 14
United Kingdom The Kennel Club, 1-4 Clarges Street, London W1Y 8AB
United States of America American Kennel Club, 51 Madison Avenue, New York, NY 10010: The United Kennel Club Inc, 100 East Kilgore Road, Kalamazoo, MI 49001-5598

Further Reading
Canine terminology, H Spira, Harper & Row, Sydney, 1982
Dog Steps, R P Elliot, Howell Book House, New York
The Dobermann, Hilary Harmer, Foyles, UK, 1968
The Doglopaedia, J M Evans and Kay White, Henston, UK, 1985
Genetics and the Inheritance of Coat Colour in the Dobermann, Jimmy Richardson, Dobermann Club Yearbook, UK, 1978
Practical Dog Breeding and Genetics, Eleanor Frankling, Popular Dogs, London
The Conformation of the Dog, R H Smyth, Popular Dogs, London

Glossary of dog terminology

AKC: American Kennel Club

Angulation: Angle formed by the bones, mainly the shoulder, forearm, stifle and hock.

Anorchid: Male animal without testicles.

Anus: Anterior opening under the tail.

Backline: Topline of dog from neck to tail.

Bite: The position of the teeth when the mouth is shut.

Bitch: Female dog.

Breastbone: Bone running down the middle of the chest, to which all but the floating ribs are attached; sternum.

Breeder: Someone who breeds dogs.

Brisket: The forepart of the body below the chest between the forelegs.

Brood bitch: Female used for breeding.

Bull neck: A heavy neck, well-muscled.

Canine: Animal of the genus canis which includes dogs, foxes, wolves and jackals.

Canines: The four large teeth in the front of the mouth, two upper and two lower next to incisors.

Carpals: Bones of the pastern joints

Castrate: To surgically remove the testes of a male.

Cow-hocked: Hocks turned inwards.

Croup: The rear part of the back above the hind legs.

Crown: The highest part of the head: the top of the skull.

Cryptorchid: A male dog with neither testicle descended.

Cull: To eliminate unwanted puppies.

Dam: Mother of the puppies.

Dew claw: Extra claw on the inside lower portion of legs.

Elbow: The joint between the upper arm and forearm.

Femur: The large heavy bone of the thigh between the pelvis and stifle joint.

Flank: Side of the body between the last rib and the hip.

Forearm: Front leg between elbow and pastern.

Foreface: Front part of the head before the eyes; the muzzle.

Handler: A person who handles (shows) a dog at dog shows, field trials or obedience tests.

Hare foot: A long narrow foot.

Haw: A third eyelid at the inside corner of the eye.

Heat: An alternative word for 'season' in bitches.

Heel: Command by handler to keep the dog close to his heel.

Heel free: Command whereby the dog must walk to heel without a lead.

Height: Vertical measurements from withers to ground.

Hip dysplasia: Malformation of the ball of the hip joint.

Hock: Lower joint of the hind-legs.

Hucklebones: Top of the hip bones.

Humerus: Bone of the upper arm.

In-breeding: The mating of closely related dogs of the same standard.

Incisors: Upper and lower front teeth between the canines.

Ischium: Hipbone.

In season: On heat, ready for mating.

Inter-breeding: The breeding together of different varieties.

Jowls: Flesh of lips and jaws.

Level bite: The upper and lower teeth edge to edge.

Line breeding: The mating of related dogs within a line or family to a common ancestor, ie dog to grand-dam or bitch to grand-sire.

Litter: The pups from one whelping.

Loin: Either side of the vertebrae column between the last rib and hip bone.

Mate: The sex act between the dog and bitch.

Milk teeth: First teeth. (Puppies lose these at four to six months.)

Molars: Rear teeth.

Monorchid: A male animal with only one testicle in the scrotum.

Muzzle: The head in front of the eyes, including nose, nostril and jaws.

Nose: The ability to scent.

Occiput: The rear of the skull.

Oestrum: The period during which a bitch has her menstrual flow and can be mated.

Out-crossing: The mating of unrelated individuals of the same breed.

Overshot: Front teeth (incisors) of the upper jaw overlap and do not touch the teeth of the lower jaw.

Pads: The tough, cushioned soles of the feet.

Paper foot: A flat foot with thin pads.

Pastern: Foreleg between the carpus and the digits.

Patella: Knee cap composed of cartilage at the stifle joint.

Pedigree: The written record of the names of a dog's ancestors.

Pelvis: Set of bones attached to the end of the spinal column.

Pigeon-toed: With toes pointing.

Police dog: A dog trained for police work (often the German Shepherd Dog).

Puppy: A dog up to 12 months of age.

Quarters: The two hindlegs.

Scapula: The shoulder blade.

Scissor bite: The outside of the lower incisors touches the inner side of the upper incisors.

Second thigh: The part of the hindquarters from stifle to hock.

Seeing eye dog: A guide dog for the blind (in the USA).

Set on: Insertion or attachment of tail or ears.

Set up: Posed so as to make the most of the dog's appearance for the show ring.

Sire: A dog's male parent.

Soft-mouthed: Able to carry retrieved game in the mouth without damaging it.

Spay: To surgically remove the ovaries to prevent conception.

Splay feet: Feet with toes spread wide.

Standard: The standard of perfection for a breed.

Sternum: The brisket or breast bone.

Stifle: The hindlegs above the hock.

Stop: Indentation between the eyes.

Stud: Male used for breeding.

Tail set: How the base of the tail sets on the rump.

Thigh: Hindquarters from hip to stifle.

Throatiness: An excess of loose skin under the throat.

Topline: The dog's outline from just behind the withers to the tail set.

Type: The characteristic qualities distinguishing a breed; the embodiment of the standards essentials.

Under-coat: The soft, furry wool beneath the outer hair, giving protection against cold and wet.

Undershot: The front teeth of the lower jaw projecting or overlapping the front teeth of the upper jaw.

Upper arm: The humerus or bone of the foreleg between shoulder blade and the forearm.

Vent: The anal opening.

Whelp: The act of giving birth.

Withers: The highest point of the shoulders just behind the neck.

Wrymouth: Mouth in which the lower jaw does not line up with the upper.